"Sophia Ruffin-V
she doesn't just preach a sermon—you feel like you're walking through a battlefield with a trusted friend who's already come out the other side with scars that shine like medals. This book is for anyone who has ever been blindsided by life, betrayed by circumstance, or buried under the weight of unanswered prayers. With raw vulnerability and prophetic clarity, Sophia ushers you into a realm where God's goodness breaks the rules and redefines the outcome. Every chapter is soaked in glory, grit, and gospel truth. This isn't a feel-good book—it's a faith-fight manual. Get ready to weep, war, and win. *It will be God or it will be God*—and this book proves it."

Tomi Arayomi, founder, RIG Nation; president,
Tomi Arayomi Ministries

"*It Will Be God* is an awe-inspiring, jaw-dropping testament to the reality of God's goodness. Each page bursts with faith-building insights that will inspire you to trust more deeply in God's overwhelming, miraculous goodness like never before. This book will leave you uplifted, renewed, and truly in awe."

Apostle John Eckhardt, bestselling author,
Prayers That Route Demons

"We live in a world constantly flooded with bad reports and evil attacks. In times like these, we need continual reminders of the goodness and majesty of God to live victoriously. I believe this book is a powerful remedy for hopelessness, fear, and calamity. Sophia Ruffin-Wilson has masterfully penned a testimony—an intimate and compelling account of her victory journey—that will anchor your mind and position you for breakthrough and triumph."

Ryan LeStrange, founder, Global Hub and ATL Hub
Church; author, *Overcoming Spiritual Attack*

"Sophia Ruffin-Wilson's life is living proof of what only God's power can do! *It Will Be God* challenges you to believe beyond what you can see. It serves as a clarion call to trust His sovereign plan and believe God for the impossible."

Pastor Medina Pullings, mentor and speaker;
CEO, Jesus Girl

IT WILL BE GOD

IT WILL BE GOD

SOPHIA RUFFIN-WILSON

LIVE IN THE
JAW-DROPPING
REALITIES OF
GOD'S GOODNESS

Chosen

a division of Baker Publishing Group
Minneapolis, Minnesota

Published by Chosen Books
Minneapolis, Minnesota
ChosenBooks.com

Chosen Books is a division of
Baker Publishing Group, Grand Rapids, Michigan

Printed in the United States of America

Library of Congress Cataloging-in-Publication Control Number: 2025010103

ISBN 9780800773144 (paper)
ISBN 9780800773212 (casebound)
ISBN 9781493450527 (ebook)

Cover design by Micah Kandros Design

Author is represented by the literary agency of Embolden Media Group, LLC.

Baker Publishing Group publications use paper produced from sustainable forestry practices and post-consumer waste whenever possible.

25 26 27 28 29 30 31   7 6 5 4 3 2 1

I dedicate this book to my mother (1955–2021), who taught me about a man named Jesus. You taught me to hold on to Jesus even if I had only a little piece of a string left, to never let go. You shared with me the beauty of serving God, trusting God, and longing for the glory. Thank you for imparting in me the love of God, which has kept me during the season I lost you. I pray that this book and my perseverance are a reflection of how well you raised me.

To my late grandmother who loved,
supported, and believed in me.

CONTENTS

FOREWORD

You didn't just stumble upon this book—you were *led* to it. And let me tell you something, if you're holding this book in your hands right now, then I need you to understand this: God is about to flip the script in your life. This isn't just another feel-good devotional or some watered-down inspiration. No, this is a spiritual wake-up call. It's a divine declaration. And my friend Sophia Ruffin-Wilson came in hot with a message straight from the throne room of heaven: *It will be God or it will be God.*

Let that settle in your spirit for a minute.

As someone who knows what it's like to come back from brokenness, I can tell you this truth: God is still in the business of restoring, healing, and showing out on behalf of His kids. And that's what you're going to feel from the very first page of this book. You're going to feel seen. You're going to feel understood. But most importantly, you're going to feel the presence of God stirring something deep within you. Sophia reminds us that Yahweh, the I Am of Exodus 3:14, still remembers what He said. Even if we forgot. Even if we drifted. Even if we doubted. God remembers His promises.

What I love about Sophia—and what you're about to ex-perience—is that she doesn't just give you a pretty message. She gives you the raw, the real, and the redemptive. She'll walk with you through the dark places and point you toward the light. She's been through the fire, and now she's coming back for you with a word that says, "Let's go, we're getting out of this together."

She doesn't just inspire your *feelings*—she ignites your *faith*.

This is your invitation to break free from everything that's tried to stop you. It's your cue to hit the reset button and return to the factory settings of who God originally created you to be. It's a blueprint for those who are tired of plan B and ready to trust God for plan G—God's plan. You'll dive into the reality of open heavens, bloodline-breaking anoint-ings, and a supernatural mindset shift that says, "I'm not settling. I'm stepping into everything God has for me."

Let me make it plain: You are not too far gone. You are not too broken. And it's not too late. This book will remind you that the fight is already fixed and your victory is already in motion.

Turn each page with expectation. Read this like your next breakthrough depends on it—because it just might. Get ready to walk away with bold faith, renewed strength, and a fire in your belly that says, "Come hell or high water, it will be God."

Let's go!

With love and fire,
Pastor Kimberly "Real Talk Kim" Jones,
pastor, author, hope dealer

AUTHOR'S NOTE

It Will Be God contains an intimate look at the most recent years of my life. As such, this work contains the recounting of a medical emergency and the resulting loss of my mother. Please know that this topic was shared with the utmost care and vulnerability. I share my experience openly with the hope of not triggering anyone who may be navigating their own loss.

INTRODUCTION

It will be God or it will be God.®

Breakthrough is possible. Your life can change beyond recognition. You can move into a realm of the jaw-dropping realities of God's goodness in which you experience good news after good news after good news. You can ditch the keys to—and the extended warranty on—the struggle bus. Sounds too good to be true? It's not. It will be God! He will open unexpected doors of healing, wholeness, opportunity, and provision.

Ask me how I know.

I am living proof of the jaw-dropping realities of God's goodness. You might be thinking, *Sophia, that's not my reality.* Well, it wasn't mine either! See, like the prophet Amos, I did not inherit a prophetic mantle (Amos 7:14). In fact, I was minding my business and living in rebellion (*let me tell the truth and shame the devil!*) before God plucked me up, changed my life, and set me on a mind-blowing course of prophetic alignment. My spiritual testimony is enough to prove that God is good all the time—and all the time God is good. But there's more to my story.

I don't call myself the Comeback Kid for nothing. For some time now, I have been on this journey of watching the hand of God at work in my life. If you follow me on social media or have heard me speak, you know that I share openly about the ways God has been good to me. I've shared how I went from broke to multiple streams of income. From sleeping on a blow-up bed on my mother's floor to buying my first home. And from a nine-to-five job to full-time ministry. All glory to God!

My assignment is leading people to God.

Titles don't matter to me. But if you need one or two, I'm a prophet and preacher. I'm an out-of-the-box type of person, purposefully not fitting into any strict definition of what ministry supposedly looks like. If you follow me on social media, you know your girl Sophia uses faith, fashion, and fun to draw people to Jesus. I love what I do. There is nothing like seeing people saved, delivered, and set free. My calling is to the nations, and God has opened doors for me to preach throughout the United States and abroad. I am grateful for this dream life as an itinerant preacher that I never imagined as possible for *me*.

If God did nothing else in my life, I would be blessed and highly favored. However, He did more. There was a recent season when I was living in the realm of the unexpected, what I've called my out-the-blue moments, my Amos 9:13 season. I was in a supernatural season of good news after good news after good news. Everywhere I turned God was blessing me or opening a door or showing me favor in some way I wasn't looking for.

During this time, He offered divine insight, encouragement, and clarity. I experienced moments when He downloaded an overflow of practical wisdom. God reminded me that my future is secured, that every word spoken over my life before the foundations of the world served a purpose.

He taught me not to get caught up in my emotions, but to embrace Scriptures like 1 Peter 4:7; 5:8; 2 Timothy 4:5; and Proverbs 3:5. I kept hearing *"Sophia, be sober. Be of a sound mind. Trust me."*

For years, God had assured me of His purpose for my life and the original intent in which I was sent into the earth. But my Amos 9:13 season stretched me—and my faith. Daily I had to lean into His goodness and intentionally pursue being in His presence. God taught me how to practice His presence and how to live under an open heaven, a concept I'll explore more fully in another chapter.

To put it briefly for now, I believe living under an open heaven means a heightened ability to hear and obey God. When I act, I receive favor. What was once impossible becomes reality. And it's a time when God is moving faster than I can pray (Isaiah 65:24). Spiritually, it's like having a strong Wi-Fi signal. Everything I do is easier and more productive because I'm connected to God, my wireless link to heaven. That connection powers intimacy with Him, answered prayers, and breakthroughs.

I want that same relationship for you—one of hearing God, obeying Him, then prospering in the outcome. I want that goodness for you. But before you grab these keys and take off, I want to share with you how this moment came to be.

In early 2021, in the midst of good news after good news, my life hit rock bottom. I spiraled to the lowest level ever, and didn't think it was humanly possible to recover. My mother went into cardiac arrest on April 7, 2021. How could this be happening? We'd just buried my maternal grandmother at the end of March, a week earlier. Double grief overwhelmed me. The loss of one and the sudden threat of losing the other of the two most important women in my life left me in a pile of devastation. This was not the one thing on the heels of another I'd taken Amos 9:13 to mean.

The day lives rent-free in my head. I can recall its fear-inducing details like they happened yesterday. The rising sun peeked through my bedroom windows, throwing beams of light across the ceiling just as the sound of a loud bang jolted me upright. I jumped up, trying to locate the origin of the noise. I looked down, realizing that my phone had vibrated off the nightstand and landed on the floor. Its muffled dance of urgency shook me fully awake. My heart pounded. My palms dripped with sweat. I reached for the phone.

Lord, please help, I prayed.

Weeks of late-night phone calls and early morning scares prior to my grandmother's passing had left me shaken. A form of trauma had attached itself to the mere ringing of my phone. I quickly glanced at the clock, nearly 6:00 a.m. This was not a casual call, especially since everyone knows I am not an early riser.

"It's your mother. She's not breathing, and the ambulance is on the way."

As the words about my mother's condition bullied their way through the phone's receiver, pummeling my heart, all time stopped. My breath caught in my throat. My entire life was falling apart, *again*.

After all of my recent out-the-blue-themed preaching and testifying, what was happening to my mother was a whole other kind of out-the-blue. I'd preached about God's delivering us from nightmare situations, and how He's positioning us for fields of dreams. But nothing prepared me for the nightmare of my grandmother's death or my mother's health crisis.

I jumped into action. Yet I don't remember hanging up or much else in that moment besides grabbing sweatpants and dashing out the door. I don't know how I made it to my mother's home safely because tears blinded my vision as I repeated the name of Jesus while speeding down the road.

Looking back, I believe angels and goodness guided me safely to my mama's house.

When I arrived, she was already in the ambulance. I rode with my godmother as she closely followed the vehicle. I was so out of it; I didn't even realize that the sirens weren't on as we approached the hospital. I'm glad I didn't notice.

Back then, I thought a silent ambulance meant a patient is beyond help. I now know that's not always the case. Sometimes a siren is purposefully turned off. According to the U.S. Fire Administration, "The use of emergency vehicles' lights and siren does not save clinically significant amounts of time, and it is associated with an increase in ambulance crashes."[1] Because of the accident risks, turning them off could increase safety in an already stress-inducing situation.

By the time we arrived, not only was my mama in cardiac arrest, but the attending staff told us she had an anoxic brain injury. No oxygen was flowing to her brain. Her organs were beginning to shut down. My level of shock deepened as they shared that she was considered brain-dead.

I hyperventilated each time I tried processing their updates. Zero brain activity? Not my mother, "Baby D"! She was my favorite human being, the one I loved beyond words. Nothing made sense. My thoughts scattered as the numbness of reality began to settle in. I am usually so strong. I was usually the sound, faithful one; however, in a matter of seconds everything I knew went blank. I couldn't think. Shock after shock rippled through me. Fresh tears stung my eyes. I dazed into space, wondering what God could make of this situation.

I would soon find out.

After visiting my mama for weeks in the ICU and receiving prognosis after prognosis, I had nowhere to turn for a different medical opinion or treatment option. Doctors told me my mother was dying; with zero brain activity she was already considered dead. She was on a ventilator, then had a tracheotomy placed down her throat. It was traumatic watching as she underwent intense medical care for more than ninety days.

Finally, the medical staff came to us for a decision: have them turn off the breathing machine or allow our mother to continue in her current condition. I did not want to choose either option, but the medical staff pushed my family and me to decide. At that moment I knew that if I made the wrong decision, it would impact my mental, emotional, physical, and spiritual life.

I sought counsel from doctors, influential leaders, family, and friends, but no one gave me the answers I was seeking. They provided wisdom, but I still felt stuck in the valley of indecision. I had no sense of hope or clear direction. I had no new path forward given the reality of the situation. But God met me at that crossroad.

One evening, I found myself frustrated and overwhelmed with it all and screamed at the top of my lungs, "God, help me! Please help me!"

Generally, I can be somewhat loud. This time I had the volume on max frustration. I was tired of the dead-end answers. God was going to hear me this time like He never had before. The dam of numbness I'd experienced for weeks before gave way to sobs; I needed a response. Shivers of panic raced through my body. Balled up into the fetal position, I was at the end of my rope, desperately pleading for help. I cried like an inconsolable baby. I wanted my mama. I wanted Father God to answer me.

Suddenly a calm, settled voice said, *"Sophia,* it will be God or it will be God. *There will be no other options. It will be a win-win situation. Trust me."*

I immediately relaxed. Though tears still blanketed my face, something within me clicked. Peace settled on me, and

I felt a charge of victory. I felt certain and assured. I felt God. I knew that if I approached the crossroad with faith to believe it will be God, then the weight of regret, guilt, and fear would be arrested. I knew that if I believed it will be God, the outcome—no matter what it looked like now—would be successful, and He who began a good work would complete it (Philippians 1:6).

Having faith to believe it will be God orchestrating a win-win situation gives us the confidence, hope, faith, and courage to make the right decisions in the most difficult circumstances. Believing it will be God gives us the strength to endure post-decision seasons when everything seemingly goes wrong before going right. However, believing it will be God is not a quick fix, and you may not get instant gratification. God's answer may not be what you prayed for. I prayed for my mama to live—and thrive. My loss is heaven's gain.

Believing it will be God means sticking with God and trusting His Word through what David called "the valley of the shadow of death" (Psalm 23:4 ESV). (For the purpose of this book, that valley includes any type of devastating situation.)

I'm telling you that moment of hearing God's reassuring voice and adopting an it-will-be-God mentality have changed my life forever. Since I began my journey of declaring, "It will be God," I have seen the supernatural hand of God break barriers. Doors have been opened, and incredible favor has been released upon my life. I even met and married the most amazing and caring gentleman. He's the handsomest and kindest man I've ever met! He treats me like a woman, and I love that for me and him. If you have followed my story from one of my first self-published books, *Feminine Progression*, or heard my testimony online, then you know this all had to be God. And, yes, it was out the blue! I'll share all about our pleasantly surprising romance and #WilsonWeddingBliss in a later chapter.

This book is the overflow of everything I learned about God and His ultimate position in our lives as we face the impossible. I am unaware of your point of desperation. I do not know your current challenges. But I know this: God already has a plan for your life. He knows exactly what He's doing. He will finish what He's begun in you and get the glory for it.

I've written this book to fire up your faith. There are other books out there that offer pacifier-level peace for spiritual babes. Not this one. It offers sustenance, blessed assurance for maturing you—and your faith! Even if you're a new believer, you will grow up while reading it. This book will stir your faith and challenge you to believe that everything that's ordained for your life will be all God's doing and it will be marvelous in your eyes (Psalm 118:23). And even those things the enemy throws your way will work together for your good!

You might be thinking, *Nah, Sophia. I love God. This evil I'm dealing with is not from Him!* Do you know it can still be used by God for your good? Romans 8:28 (MSG) reminds us, "We can be so sure that every detail in our lives of love for God is worked into something good." Get ready to discover how you can live in the jaw-dropping goodness of God's realities!

When your back is against the wall, there is no other option: It will be God; it must be God. You must come to believe that. Let it become the anthem for your life.

Only One Sure Option

Throughout the pages of this book, we will look at the promises of God concerning you, which are always yes and amen (2 Corinthians 1:20). Yahweh remembers what He said. *Yahweh* is the name of God in Exodus 3:14. During a divine encounter at the burning bush, Moses asked about God's name. "And God said to Moses, 'I AM WHO I AM'" (Exodus 3:14 NKJV). That name is translated as Yahweh. The Israelites would soon discover God had not forgotten about them. He remembered His promise to protect, deliver, and bless them, sending Moses to lead them to the Promised Land. In a later chapter I share more about how Yahweh remembers us. For now, just know that God remembers His promises.

God remembers what He's said to *you*. But do you? Sometimes we just have to remind ourselves or be reminded of the things God has spoken over our lives. If you need a refresher on what God is saying to you in this season, don't worry, family. I got you.

If you are like I was when all of this started, you are at a crossroad. You need to make some decisions. I want to walk with you toward the lighted pathway, which becomes clear when you settle in your spirit that only one outcome is possible. Victory, breakthrough, deliverance, healing, provision— whatever is stored in God's riches—is yours. Because all God does is win. All God does is deliver. All God does is heal and restore. All God does is cause you to prosper. There is no other option.

If you have been feeling a little unsure because of the dark place you have been in lately, I got you on that too! We will press into what we can do when everything around us seems dark. You know what I'm talking about. That moment when you're suddenly caught off guard by unexpected calamity and can't see your way out, can't imagine what's in front of you, and you are unwilling to turn around to see what's behind you. No worries. This book offers needed light for you to see that you're almost at the end of that tunnel! You may be in deep right now, but you're coming out on the other side victorious! *It will be God or it will be God.*

We are also going to activate a supernatural reset button. Sometimes life seems to act up like an old cell phone.

Sometimes you just need to hit reset, returning it back to its factory settings, for it to act right. It's time for your heart and mind to act right! And that means you'll need to live like you know God is your only option. I'll show you how to live that way.

We also will explore the concept of an open heaven and what it's like to stand under it. Let me tell you something: There is nothing like that feeling of owning your place as one of God's chosen ones who knows what the end is going to be. It's the assurance and safety of knowing that you are with God—and have access to His provision. One who knows the faithfulness of God. Who knows without a doubt that God is faithful until the end and that He never fails. Chosen ones dwell under an open heaven. *Dwell* simply means to occupy, reside, or live. Imagine cohabitating with God Himself!

Finally, what we accomplish in God along our journey to the win-win outcome will not be sustained if we lack faith. Faith is the prerequisite to remaining under an open heaven. Living under an open heaven will take work and break some generational things off our bloodlines! So we will spend time identifying and breaking out of those things from past generations that have hindered you. For you to fully live out the original intent for your life, generational sins and curses must stop with you. You are the bloodline-curse breaker. Trust God for a bloodline-changing anointing. And get ready to live in the jaw-dropping realities of God's goodness.

Let God Be God

Listen, family, something is getting ready to happen. Whatever pressure you have been under, whatever things you have been worried about or concerned about, you're going to feel so much better by the time you finish reading this book. You're going to know God better and experience His peace.

You're going to close this book feeling the momentum of God, like you can accomplish anything. It's time to throw out the plan B's. You need to decide that *it will be God or it will be God*, and there are literally no other options. The Bible says in Zechariah 4:6 that it is not by might nor by power but by the Spirit of the living God! There is none beside Him.

God has some jaw-dropping moments already in the queue for you. Blessings, pressed down and running over (Luke 6:38), are just waiting to be released to you. It is time for you to step aside from trying to do everything from your own strength. Let God be God so that He can lead you toward a life of goodness.

I don't know about you, but I'm excited about what's about to happen for you! It may be hard right now, but trust me: Shortly, it will all make sense. You are being perfected both naturally and spiritually.

I just know you picked up this book seeking change. Reading it and coming this far indicates that you are ready for a faith lift. You are ready to see what's going to happen when you accept the fact that the fight is fixed. Where you are going, it won't be about who you know or whose elbow you rub. It will be about the Spirit of God within you—the one who knows all your deeds and deets. When you trust that God has you, your future will roll out perfectly according to His plan.

Declaring, and more importantly accepting, that it will only be God opens a new level of understanding and opportunity. I'm excited about all that is about to happen in your life as you adopt this new mindset. So let's dive into the promise of His Word with expectancy. *It will be God or it will be God!*

1
OUT OF THE BLUE

"IS THERE A WORD from the Lord?"

I am committed to hearing—and delivering—a timely word from God (2 Timothy 4:2). I stay ready, so I don't have to get ready. I spend hours preparing to be used by God. I yield to Holy Spirit's promptings. But nothing could have prepared me for the out-of-the-blue prophecy I shared that turned my life upside down! The bottom line: Expect the unexpected.

Have you ever experienced something catching you off guard or by surprise? You may have even said to yourself or to others, "Wow, that happened out of the blue." I never paid much attention to the statement. I would just automatically refer to anything unexpected as an out-of-the-blue encounter or moment. I never gave it any thought. Now that I think about it, I'm not sure whether I heard this statement from others and adopted it, or I was taught that this was something that many people said when the unexpected happened in their lives. In either case, I found it funny how this same statement was used to describe an unexpected happening whether it was good or bad. Out of the blue, in my view, was a neutral statement.

I can recall the day the statement gained significance in my life. "Out the blue," how I say it, was a cliché to me when I received a message from one of my favorite preachers, Dr. Medina Pullings. Her team reached out to me about being a special guest on *The Medina Pullings Show* on the Word Network. I was overjoyed by the opportunity, and just grateful for the invitation.

During the segment, she asked me what word I was sensing from the Lord. My mind went blank. I forgot everything I thought I was going to say. Gazing around the room, I saw the color blue everywhere. It was Christmastime, and her set had been decorated for the season. The blue ornaments stood out to me in an unusual way. Within seconds, out of my mouth came these words:

> "Get ready for God to bless you out the blue. You will look up and see the answers to your prayers finally coming to pass. It will be out of nowhere, making a sudden appearance."

After making that decree, I started experiencing out-the-blue blessings. Out-the-blue checks. Out-the-blue notifications of Cash App payments. Out-the-blue connections. Out-the-blue doors of opportunity. It was as if God was let loose to have so much fun because my faith to believe had unlocked these supernatural suddenlies—the blessing and goodness of God. I was experiencing the jaw-dropping realities of God's goodness—a realm of good news after good news after good news!

Testimonies reached me. People who made the same out-the-blue declaration had out-the-blues happening for them. God used this word to unlock a miraculous faith movement all by itself in my life and in the lives of the thousands of people I minister to every day. When I began to meditate more on this prophetic moment, it unlocked my faith even more, and I simply began to enjoy God more and more. What a time!

Although those were positive out-the-blues, I had experiences with unexpected out-the-blues that caught me off guard. What I discovered is life happens; things will hit us unexpectedly; however, God is the same and nothing catches

Him by surprise. I had to understand that God has a prepared solution for every unexpected moment.

Let that sink in. Wherever you are right now, I don't want you to miss this. *God has a prepared solution for every unexpected moment.* I promise if you keep reading, you will discover this truth for yourself. Out-the-blue blessings of God can happen in your life. And you can live in God's jaw-dropping realities.

Pretty quickly, the phrase "out the blue" lost its neutrality for me. Through this experience, the statement became bigger; the significance of the phrase enlarged. It was as if God put a magnifying glass on the words and each word came to life. Out. Of. The. Blue. Wow!

The very phrase I was haphazardly using to describe an unexpected moment—good or bad—became active and positive no matter what it looked like on the surface, because God turns everything around for our good (Genesis 50:20; Romans 8:28). It was as if God blew His breath on this statement, and it became a real, living, and tangible word—something of substance I could attach my faith to. And not only me but all those for whom this word became real. The power behind it produced a movement.

The movement hasn't stopped. There's still an anointing on the decree. That's why I wrote this book. I believe every reader can trust God to move into the out-the-blue realm. *You* can live in the jaw-dropping realities of God's goodness.

Trust and believe: The more aware I became of what was happening, the more I witnessed God blow on these words to unlock miraculous moments in my life. It became the word of the Lord for that season of my life. My faith was activated, and I dared to believe that if anything good could happen in my life, it would happen and it would be God. He'd do it to get the glory from it.

The Bible declares in Hebrews 11:6 (KJV), "Without faith it is impossible to please him: for he that cometh to God must believe that he is, and that he is a rewarder of them that diligently seek him."

One word in this Scripture triggered something within me and initiated a response. We know God as a lot of things. However, when I tapped into how this verse reveals God as being a rewarder, I was stirred. I began imagining the rewards coming from God, and how my faith to believe could please Him. I wanted to know more about faith. How to have faith in every season, without my emotions interfering. I wanted to learn how to believe God regardless of the season I faced. I wanted to be surefooted, which I define as spiritually grounded and confident. But not only to please God; honestly, I also wanted the reward of the Lord. Listen, I want everything that God has for me. How about you? If there is a reward for diligently seeking Him, I want it. If faith pleases God, I want God-pleasing faith.

So I began digging into unlocking the meaning of this new level of faith I believe God was calling me up to. I dug more deeply into the Word of God. I fasted, prayed, and sought counsel from my mentors. What I discovered is that my faith has nothing to do with my emotions. That faith isn't a feeling. *Faith* is an action word that requires me to remain unmovable and surefooted through every season. Regardless of how I felt, I had to continue to believe God and His Word. This revelation infused me with indescribable strength and peace. I wanted God to know that I would diligently seek Him during every season of my life.

Since I sought the meaning of that new level of faith, I have maintained a consistent focus that if God be for me, nothing can stand against me (Romans 8:31). That type of childlike faith to love God, seek God, pursue God, and trust God at all times unlocked a fresh anointing in my life.

Living in the jaw-dropping realities of God's goodness requires faith. We must have faith. We must believe God and take Him at His word. We must believe Him for what He's saying! If God says He will never leave us or forsake us, then we must believe that even when we don't feel Him.

Again, faith isn't a feeling.

There are days and seasons when I don't feel God, but my faith that He lives in me and He is with me keeps me confident in my walk with Him. If God says nothing can separate us from His love (Romans 8:38–39), then we must believe nothing can come between us and God. The Word of God is powerful when you read it in faith. When you believe it because you are sure that if God said it, then it is so.

Listen, we don't go to church, prophesy, speak in tongues, or pray, not to believe. We believe the Word of God. And the Word of God is true. Hebrews 11:1 (KJV) says, "Now faith is the substance of things hoped for, the evidence of things not seen."

Being consistent is a key to strong faith. We can't have faith one moment and doubt the next. So I focused on consistency. I exercised my faith by expecting and believing God for out-of-the-blue moments. Every day, I'd wake up and look for ways God might surprise me. Would it be a fresh revelation as I studied His Word? Would it be an encouraging word from someone in my circle? Would I come across a stranger I could bless or encourage? Would it be an unexpected tangible blessing or miracle?

God has infinite ways to bring His goodness into our lives. Still today, I experience out-the-blue moments because the blessing and goodness of God—His suddenlies—don't have to be seasonal. We can expect them every day in every or any circumstance.

Out-of-the-blue is a faith movement, a diligent seeking, and an excitement to see the unseen, the hidden miracle, the unexpected provision released in our lives. And the unexpected encounters in which God uses us to usher out-the-blue moments into other peoples' lives. Never forget that you are blessed to be a blessing (Genesis 12:2). That's a dimension of faith we sometimes overlook, especially during seasons of adversity.

Psalm 139:16 (NLT) says, "Every day of my life was recorded in your book. Every moment was laid out before a single day had passed." This means that God has already recorded my days. He has plans for me that have not come to pass yet. So if God has recorded my days and knows the plans He has for me (Jeremiah 29:11), then there are some things in the realm of the Spirit that must come to pass in my life and manifest physically, or in the natural. This revelation gave me peace and comfort, and I began to yield more to God's plans being yes and amen (2 Corinthians 1:20) for my life.

So even though things may be a surprise to us—whether good or bad—nothing really is happening out of the blue. And God *can* release a Romans 8:28 anointing on *anything*. And while the phrase worked for me as God began revealing to me His truth about all the things that happen in my life, I don't casually use the phrase when I am caught by surprise anymore. I know that what feels out of the blue is really a sign that my life is coming more and more into alignment with God's perfect plan for me and my future.

Living in this experience, testifying of it, and leaning in closer to God to hear what's next have increased my awareness of how out-of-the-blue moments can be activated in my life and in the lives of others. They are the tangible elements of the it-will-be-God revelation in action. God has unlocked this mystery for me, and I am eager to share with you how to experience the beauty of out-of-the-blue moments in your life. It's all about the exchange.

The Exchange

Each out-of-the-blue moment brings with it breakthrough, victory, and expectation. Ephesians 3:20 (NKJV) tells us God "is able to do exceedingly abundantly above all that we ask or think, according to the power that works in us." To get to the place where His power works within us, an exchange is needed.

You must be willing to exchange your anxieties, worries, and fears for additional, intentional prayer.

You have been stressed, worried, and anxious trying to work things out and figure them out for yourself. You may even have been able to get away with doing your own thing, and when that didn't work out quite as you planned, you returned to your prayer and devotion time. The problem with this is that you are asking God to do things that your current devotion is not able to keep you in. God is trying to make sure that in this season you have the capacity to be devoted. This is where the exchange comes into play. You must be prayed up! And I'm not talking about the asking kind of prayers. I'm talking about the prayer time when you create real and meaningful space for God.

If you create space for God, He'll create a stage for you.

Any revelation of God shifts our life for the better. One of my favorite statements I've been declaring is this: "As long as you have a revelation, you will have an open door." Taking it to heart, I began to lean more into God, learning new ways to practice the presence, and tap into the place where God reveals Himself to me more and more. The more I seek God, the more *He* reveals Himself. Let me tell you how I know.

A few years ago, I had a lull in my schedule. My itinerary books were closed, and I was enjoying a break from preaching and traveling. During that time, the Lord was really on me about spending more time with Him, being anchored in

Him. Now, God was blessing, and things were going well; however, I felt a void, which led me to a tremendous burden for prayer. I know this was God's divine orchestration. He wanted me to Himself; *He* wanted to be El Shaddai in my life, more than enough. In Genesis 17:1, God reveals Himself to Abram as the El Shaddai, the Almighty God who is more than enough. As He was then, God is still seeking to be more than enough to His people.

God stirred a hunger for Him within me so that the only thing that fulfilled me was being in harmony with Holy Spirit. I knew I needed to make space and time to cry out to God, to connect to my Creator without it being a need or want. I just needed time being fulfilled by God's presence alone. I would say to God, "I want You because I just want You." I didn't want what God had; I wanted Him. I hungered for His presence more than any presents, physical manifestations of answered prayer. I needed His presence and wanted to be in a place where His presence was more than enough.

Naturally, we experience a yearning for someone's presence when dating or married. We just want to be around that person, hanging on their every word. We want to be nearby, enjoying conversation or silence. It's more than enough to be with our beloved.

When I answered His call to come away for this time with Him, the kind of prayer that came rushing out of me was louder than usual. I'd roar, groan, and pray in the Spirit, unable to put English words to what was happening in the Spirit.

Have you ever groaned while praying? It's different, but biblical! Groaning is a way Holy Spirit helps us pray. Romans 8:26 says, "In the same way, the Spirit helps us in our weakness. We do not know what we ought to pray for, but the Spirit himself intercedes for us through wordless groans."

Jesus groaned in the Spirit twice after learning of the death of Lazarus (John 11:33, 38 KJV).

Groans helped me grow my devotional life. Like never before, I yielded to God, giving Him more time than I was giving to anyone or anything else. Yes, I was praying, but unlike other times of prayer, I was not asking God to do anything. And without my asking, He began taking care of my weights and burdens. He moved supernaturally into the role of a father who already knew exactly what I needed. Then all of a sudden—no—out of the blue, I got an unexpected call.

The call presented a tremendous opportunity for me. My immediate response was to break out in a sprint. Oh, my God! I ran. I jumped. I hopped. I shouted all through my home. Breathless, I praised God, saying, "Wow, God! I thank You." And then I paused. Wait. How did this happen?

God helped me understand that the more I prayed and spent time with Him, the more He became my rear guard (Isaiah 52:12) and moved on my behalf. A military rear guard is the troop at the rear protecting other troops' backs. You may not know exactly what God will do from one moment to the next. Yet in any situation, know that He has your back. At any moment, He can turn things in your favor.

By exchanging my anxieties, worries, and fears for additional, intentional prayer, I positioned myself for unexpected out-of-the-blue blessings. While I sought Him and His kingdom, He went about the task of adding "all these things" to me. I did not have to worry. I had only to honor my time with Him. While I was entrenched in His presence, He was putting me on the hearts of other people—decision makers, door openers, investors, and helpers.

Understanding how the exchange worked motivated me to remain steadfast in prayer. I better understood how prayer is a path to favor. Favor is about what God can do for us, in us, and through us. Favor is all about God's power being activated in or upon our lives. When you are favored by God, there is nothing you can't do. Why? Because it will be the Lord's doing, and what He does is marvelous in our eyes.

God wants to favor you. God is not just looking for you to go into a new season. Instead, He is giving you the momentum you need and an enormous amount of favor. As my apostle—John Eckhardt—puts it, a rush of favor is being released. That means that sudden favor is being poured out on you. Amos 9:13 (MSG) says, "Everything will be happening at once—and everywhere you look, blessings!" That is a rush of favor. That's when your life is coming into proper alignment.

Imagine a person who goes bowling, and each time he or she rolls the ball down the alley, it knocks a few pins down. Although another turn comes, the bowler enjoys incremental success. However, imagine a person who takes the bowling ball, squares up, hurls the ball down the lane, and knocks all the pins down at once. That's a strike, a victory. I believe a rush of favor—everything happening at once—is like a bowler getting one strike after another. Once you hit that strike in the Spirit, favor is released and everything lines up properly.

I believe you are moving from scratching the surface, or having drip-drop favor, into a rush of favor that will shift the momentum in your life as you begin to seek God first and only. When you make the exchange of devoting precious, consistent, and uninterrupted time with Him, you build momentum for God's rush of favor. Because when you pray in the Spirit with groaning and utterances that can't be understood, you are praying God's will. Yes, praying in English or your native language is great; however, when we allow Holy Spirit to make intercession for us, we pray the precise, accurate will of God for us in Christ Jesus. In

38

bowling terms, praying in the Spirit is a guaranteed strike in the life of a believer. I have initiated and experienced momentum by praying in the Spirit.

Momentum Shift

Basketball is another sport that helps us understand the effectiveness of praying in the Spirit. Fun fact: I'm a baller. Anytime players have a favorable momentum shift, everything works in their favor. Their accuracy increases. Every shot is a bucket! Nothing but net! Even if they take a horrible shot, they still hit buckets. Favor is on their side.

A momentum shift is needed for you to move into the jaw-dropping realities of God's goodness. It is time for your momentum shift. When that momentum hits you, favor will make you unstoppable. But it won't be because of your skills, education, experience, or expertise. *It will be God or it will be God!*

You must prepare yourself for the suddenly, out-of-the-blue, it-will-be-God manifestation of favor. And I know what you are thinking: *Sophia, you cannot prepare for things to happen out of the blue.*

Actually, you can.

Scar, from *The Lion King*, said it like this: "Be prepared!" In the streets, we say, "Stay ready, so you don't have to get ready." And finally, Scripture says it like this: "Be prepared in season and out of season" (2 Timothy 4:2). And "There is a time for everything, and a season for every activity under the heavens" (Ecclesiastes 3:1). To be ready for the unexpected things God will bring into your life, you must spend time with Him, getting to know His heart and mind toward you.

You can also prepare by practicing another type of exchange: Exchange your feelings of inadequacy, thoughts of being unqualified, and the stress of trying to figure everything out on your own for His plan. Jeremiah 1:5 reminds us that God knew us before we were formed. He doubles down on clarifying His good intentions toward us in Jeremiah 29:11: "'For I know the plans I have for you,' declares the LORD, 'plans to prosper you and not to harm you, plans to give you hope and a future.'"

My God! Every time I read Jeremiah 29:11, I am stirred and encouraged that indeed it will be God! You must meditate on this Scripture to maximize your out-of-the-blue journey. Believing that it will be God means resting in the knowledge and power of this word. It will be God. When you rest in God's Word concerning your future, you won't have anxiety or fear of what's next. You can simply trust that God knows exactly what He's doing, even when you don't—and that what He's doing is good! Taking this stance gives you a chance to activate your faith and please God by being unmovable regardless of what things look like in the natural. Through faith and expectancy, you can begin to see your future how God sees it.

Come on. Let's activate this power together.

Activating the Exchange

What are the things you need to release and exchange for His plans concerning you? It is time to loose the chains of paranoia, worry, and anxiety. Let go of fear and control. As you allow the Lord through prayer and Bible study to renew and steady your mind, step into a sobering moment that erases emotionally imbalanced decisions. Step into the security of God's wisdom, direction, and plan regarding your life. Proverbs 3:5–6 says, "Trust in the LORD with all your heart and lean not on your own understanding; in all your ways submit to him, and he will make your paths straight."

Practice exchanging worry for trust that God knows exactly what He is doing. The Bible says that God watches over His word to perform it (Jeremiah 1:12) and not one word will return to Him void (Isaiah 55:11).

Declare this over yourself right now. Say, "Lord, I rest in Your plan for me." Repeat it a few times, and as you repeat it, the exchange will be taking place. Release the urge to fight against the plans. The struggle and pressure will ease as you surrender. Say, "I completely rest in Your plan for me. Jeremiah 29:11 is my portion."

God's power knows no boundaries. I believe you can feel the power of God's presence working on your behalf, even through the pages. As you let go of the chains that have been holding you hostage and accept that He has a divine plan for you, your mind will be set free and your spirit opened to accept the suddenly moments of God. Your out-of-the-blue moments will come into clearer focus. You will be cautious not to throw out a dismissive or casual "Oh, that was out of the blue." Instead, you will retrain your responses to acknowledge that an it-will-be-God moment has found you.

We can miss the supernatural subtleties of God's presence, power, and provision. Prepare yourself to expect and receive them. Look for God in every situation. As you retrain your thought patterns, expectations, and responses, more of these moments will find you. They will begin to show up in your life more frequently. What is being birthed in the Spirit concerning you will be made manifest in the natural. Even if you cannot feel or see it now, the manifestation will be God's proof that He is with you.

Therefore, put your total trust in God. Lean not on your own understanding but acknowledge Him in all your ways and He will direct your path (Proverbs 3:5–6). Ask God for the gift of faith. That He would give you the capacity to hold on to His word even when it goes through a tarrying season. Though it tarry, wait, for surely it shall come to pass (Habakkuk 2:3). This supernatural focus takes practice, it takes intentionality, and it takes faith to believe God and take Him at His word. When you live in this realm, you will experience the presence of God and His power at work in your life daily.

Before we close out this chapter, let me bless you with an out-the-blue decree.

PROPHETIC DECREE

Get ready for things to happen for you out the blue. It will be sudden, unexpected, and it will catch you by surprise. You won't even see it coming. It will show up, out of nowhere, and you will know that it was God. You will find yourself running into sudden success, sudden promotion, and sudden doors. Many will ask, "How did that happen for you, and who did it for you?" You will respond, "It was out the blue, and it was God."

I declare out-the-blue phone calls, out-the-blue deliverance for your children, out-the-blue opportunities, out-the-blue miracles, out-the-blue relationships, and out-the-blue doors opening. You will be tending to your secular work, minding your business, when out the blue, God moments promote you and give you a sudden change in pay, change in position, and even change in your field. You will experience out-the-blue favor everywhere your feet tread.

You will be caught by surprise and will find yourself overwhelmed by God's goodness toward you. Out the blue, God will use people to bless you. He will use people to show up out the blue to connect and assist with what you've been trying to do for years. People you never imagined working with, speaking to, or connecting with will show up out the blue; your resources are coming.

I declare you will experience continual out-the-blue moments in your life. Your prayer life will produce the life that's been preordained. These will be God moments, miracles, and your only answer will be: It was God, and it will be God.

2

AN ANCIENT WORD

LORD, IF I GO TO THIS ALTAR, just don't embarrass me.

Those words changed my whole life. I'm saved today because of them. My salvation experience is one of those true conversion stories. The day I gave my life to the Lord, I had not been to church in a while, and I was sitting way in the back of the balcony. The pastor preached a powerful word on giving one's life to the Lord and the benefits of being born again. He declared that old things would pass away, everything could become new (2 Corinthians 5:17). As he preached, I was looking at my life, knowing I wanted that relationship with God. No. I *needed* that change of relationship in my life.

Suddenly, I felt compelled to go to the altar. I heard the voice of the Lord audibly for the first time. Yet I felt anxious and fearful; my thoughts raced. *What would giving my life to God look like?* Uncertainty gripped me. Could *I* live up to the expectations that I'd been told about?

I heard His voice again. This time, clearer and more persistent. *"Trust me with your life. For I know the plans and thoughts I have toward you."*

At that time, I did not know Scripture, so all I had were the sound of His voice and the butterflies in my belly. He spoke again: *"I'm going to give you a hope and a future. Your future is secure."* He repeatedly affirmed me.

"Lord, if I go to this altar, just don't embarrass me," I prayed.

I feared embarrassment because of my then-homosexual lifestyle. I operated in masculine expression; there wasn't anything feminine about me. The adage "Don't judge a book

47

by its cover" died when I walked into most churches. On many occasions, I noticed people staring at me. A few times pastors preached a message targeting me, using the stale joke about how God didn't make Adam and Steve but Adam and Eve. The tired joke was on them. They missed inviting a soul into God's kingdom. I can recall leaving those services embarrassed and saying to myself that I would *never* return.

Thank God for real friends! One friend persistently invited me to her church's service. So I showed up on a particular Sunday. (Let me put a pin in my testimony right here. Don't give up on your non-Christian relatives or friends. Keep leaving the door open for God to work in their lives. Tell them about Jesus! Invite them to church. Model God's love.)

Sitting in the church's balcony, for the first time I felt shame for the life I had become comfortable with. I had never felt so insecure as I did the moment when I prepared to go to the altar for prayer. The walk from the back of the balcony to the floor of the sanctuary filled me with nervousness. Under my breath, I pleaded, "Lord, please don't embarrass me. I am coming as I am."

My heart was sincerely tender, yearning for God. But the call of my future was at odds with the experience of my past. The Lord continued to affirm me of His love for me. He assured me I was loved. Just. As. I. Was. He bid me to come. I locked in with the voice of God and continued the walk of what felt like a thousand miles. As I made my way to the front, I couldn't see anyone. Time stood still, and my surroundings converged in a blur. I made it to the altar, ready for whatever was going to happen. I heard God call me, and it sounded so loving. I responded, but it wasn't a fancy, extended prayer.

It was simply "I surrender."

God heard my heartfelt confession. Apostle Tim Brinson met me at the altar and began to speak a word over my life.

Because I hadn't been to church for a while, and I didn't know Scripture, it will come as no surprise that I wasn't familiar with prophetic ministry either. Apostle Brinson moved the microphone from his mouth and leaned toward my ear. He then whispered the most powerful and truthful words I had ever heard. It was as though he'd known me for a lifetime as he prophesied everything to me: what I had been through, all that I had to overcome, and who I would become. He simultaneously spoke of my past, present, and future.

I had never experienced such a powerful expression of God's love through words and assurance. Intrigued, I stood there wondering, *Who is this God?* He'd revealed many of my secrets to the preacher, told me how much He loved me, *and* demonstrated that love by preventing my embarrassment. My heart melted; my intrigue and curiosity increased. *I must know the God who is revealing my innermost secrets this way. And more importantly, why does this God want me so much?*

I immediately became a believer.

It was completely undeniable that God knew everything about me and still wanted me. I remember going home in hot pursuit of God, with my heart buzzing with interest. I had to know this God who spoke so clearly and desperately about me. In my pursuit I was able to experience God as my healer, my deliverer, and the restorer of my soul. Through the Word and discipleship, my entire life was restored back to God's original intent and earthly purpose. God restored me inside and out, giving me beauty for ashes (Isaiah 61:3).

The Ancient Word

My conversion experience unlocked God's ancient Word to me. The ancient Word is what God spoke over us before time began. John 1:1 (KJV) says it like this: "In the beginning was the Word, and the Word was with God, and the Word was God." John 1:14 says, "The Word became flesh." God sent His Word in the form of man, His Son, Jesus. The very Word and deity that existed at the beginning of all creation became man on earth.

God has manifested so much from His Word that sometimes it's hard to believe that we have access to it. But we do. Jesus promised that Holy Spirit would come and be in us (John 14:17). The same Spirit that resided in Jesus resides in us. The same ancient Word that dwells in heaven now also dwells in us, both as the breath we breathe and via Holy Spirit in us.

We are the living manifestation of God's ancient and eternal Word. Holy Spirit was sent to remind us of what God said. His job is to lead and guide us into all truth. Holy Spirit dwells with us as the carrier of ancient answers. He helps us tap into a prayer language that unlocks the mysteries of God's Word for our lives.

Put another way, Holy Spirit is our supernatural GPS. He helps us navigate our assignment on earth as it is in heaven. In a few chapters we will dive deeper into this relationship. But for now, it's more important for you to know that you have access to the ancient realm of God's Word through the Ancient of Days (Daniel 7:9). You'll need that access to live in the jaw-dropping realities of God's goodness.

God established the ancient Word when He first said "Let there be" at creation and followed it with a declaration that everything was good (Genesis 1:31). The full force of the declaration remains—as does the ancient Word's power, purpose, and plan. In 2003, the first time I heard God audibly concerning my future, He pulled on the ancient Word from Jeremiah 29:11, spoken centuries before my birth. Yet it was true and relevant. And the same is true for you. When He declared "Let there be," you were included in the original plan and creative power of the ancient Word.

That's why I don't believe in overnight wonders. As this book's message began to form in my spirit, I realized how easy it is for us to think things are happening suddenly and swiftly for people, especially with time-lapse photos and social media highlight reels. But that's simply not true. God's Word went before us to prepare the way. We are simply catching up to meet what He's sent ahead of us.

Let me explain it a bit more.

If the Word is God (John 1:1) and God goes before us and is also with us (Deuteronomy 31:8), then His Word also goes before us and is with us. What we experience in our sense of time is the fulfillment of His ancient Word that was sent before us. His Word has been at work since long before any of us experienced it or others witnessed it. So suddenlies, long times, and other earthly time stamps are not so in the heavenlies.

God operates on an eternal continuum. But because He loves us so, He has allowed us to separate our understandings into comprehensible timing. Chunks of times broken down into minutes and hours, and weeks, months, and years help us mark our earthly existence. But thankfully, God also periodically gives us glimpses of heaven with out-the-blue moments—when His ancient Word meets our now existence. As it is in heaven! There are no coincidences, but rather, a fulfillment of the ancient Word. It takes divine intelligence to make any kind of sense of these moments. Not a problem! As believers we have the mind of Christ (1 Corinthians 2:16) and access to divine intelligence.

Divine Intelligence

Before we are ever aware of Holy Spirit in our lives or how to activate His power within us, He's already working on our behalf. He's praying for us—and through us—before we even know *how* to pray. Romans 8:26 tells us that Holy Spirit makes intercession on our behalf even when we don't know *what* to pray. His intercession comes through groanings and utterances that cannot be understood.

You know how sometimes you go to pray and you can't find the right words? Holy Spirit doesn't even worry about using the right words to go in on our behalf! He just starts making utterances. Because Holy Spirit is the same Spirit of God who was present at the release of the ancient Word of God, He already knows what the outcome is. He's not surprised by anything that happens to us and can better articulate what God has for us.

Additionally because Holy Spirit is a part of the triune God, the way that Holy Spirit prays for and through us is via the Word that has already gone forth. That's His job; it's part of the responsibility of being in our lives. Basically, this just means that the groanings and utterances are the most accurate type of prayer. He can only pray the Word as He knows it. These prayers hit the bull's-eye because who can know the mind and thoughts of God except the Spirit of God (1 Corinthians 2:11)? Because the Spirit of God is in us, we have access to God's mind and thoughts—or divine intelligence. We. Have. Access. To. Divine. Intelligence. *You* have access to divine intelligence!

Pause. Let that minister to you. Don't just read over it and move on. Fully receive it. You *can* access God's mind and thoughts, divine intelligence, through His Spirit. This realization blankets me with a sense of awe and wonder, knowing that the Spirit of the Lord can come upon me and provide access to divine intelligence.

We may never fully understand this, but we still have a divine intelligence within us. Divine intelligence is revealed through our communication with God. He searches our hearts. He unlocks the solutions that are already within us. Through divine intelligence, God releases the answers into the earth. And because we are praying in the Spirit, we can be confident that they are the right answers; we can be sure that we are praying His ancient Word. I think it's important to note here that praying in the Spirit is not just about speaking in tongues. It's about praying according to the Word of God. Praying in the Spirit is not about praying right or wrong. Praying according to divine intelligence has nothing to do with praying a specific way or withholding emotion either.

Emotions and the Word

God made us emotional beings, *and* emotions are good. They are supposed to *benefit* us. They surely can't keep us from getting to know God or growing spiritually. That's what I learned the day I gave my life to the Lord.

Walking down the aisle on my salvation day, I was filled with a number of emotions. Shame was present. Fear and anxiety tried fighting their way ahead of me. But God was spiritually reeling me in like a master fisher! I didn't have time to deal with those triple emotional hooks. I didn't have time to find the perfect words to pray. "Lord, don't embarrass me" was all that I had as I came to the altar, battling shame, fear, and anxiety. That simple prayer was enough to respond to the word He used to pull me closer.

The nature of our humanity makes us susceptible to all emotions. But we can get pulled into extreme highs and lows rather easily. When we start to feel unbalanced or overwhelming emotions, we must slow down and remember, wait, there's a word God already predestined for me, an ancient word. Sometimes, however, it's difficult to understand this revelatory truth. In my case, I'd heard enough about the love of a father that night to at least hope that God, whoever He was, would not embarrass me.

In that moment, I could not lean on my understanding of people's treatment and rejection. Instead, I had to trust that God wouldn't call me out like a person would. Instead, I chose to utilize the understanding that comes from the Spirit of God, and I understood Him to be saying, *"Come here."*

Holy Spirit gives us access to divine intelligence with which we can process spiritual things and digest them, so we are able to live them out in the earth. This process and understanding also cover our emotions. When my humanity tries to get involved with making something happen or worries about the outcome of something, I have to reach for divine intelligence.

Our humanity dictates that these emotions will come. But the Spirit and God's ancient Word are our best defenses. Fear and anxiety cannot dwell in the presence of God. God's predestined Word says that I can rest. I have the full peace of God. I must believe that if God said it, then the case is settled. That's why when I feel anxiety rising or see fear obscuring the picture of my future, I begin to pray in the Spirit. But let's be honest, it isn't always that simple. It takes daily devotion and the practicing of God's presence.

Activating the Ancient Word

Like some of you, I experience symptoms of anxiety. My hands get to sweating, my heart goes to thumping, and my thoughts get to running. Most often, anxiety kicks in when I'm not physically seeing what God said, and I have to slow down. Slowing down is a process for me. I have to take time and breathe. Slowing down to calm my anxiety requires activating the ancient Word. For me this looks like getting in the Word, searching for reminders and security. I must open my Bible, search the Scriptures, read the Word, and be reminded that God's Word is true. Before reading, I invite Holy Spirit to join me, to help me comprehend, and to assist me with retaining His Word.

I don't just rush through Scripture, reading it randomly. I read it with purpose. I read it believing that the Word of God is alive; it's the breath of God. I don't read just to teach or preach. I read the Word of God because it's the confirmation and the oil that fuel my life to stay aligned with His Spirit. Reading it helps me remain in God; His Word keeps me anchored in Him. Reading the Word has the power to transform my thinking when my fleshly emotions try to invade my life. Here's an example of what that looks like for me:

When I start feeling fear, I'm digging for the Scripture that tells me "Do not be afraid" (Isaiah 41:10 AMP). When I begin to feel anxious or worried about the future, I pull up Scriptures that remind me that my future is secure. I remind myself through the Word that if God began a good work in me, He will complete it (Philippians 1:6). I cling to the knowledge that I have been preordained, and God has already set me apart (Jeremiah 1:5).

If you're new to reading or studying the Bible, you can use different methods for finding applicable verses. Use the index in your Bible or conduct topical word searches online. For an online search, use phrases like "Bible verses about _____," "Bible promises about _____," or "What to pray when _____." Fill in the blank with the emotion or struggle you're facing. You'll get a ton of hits. Take time to read several, allowing Holy Spirit to confirm which one fits your situation. A topical Bible and a book of Bible promises are other options to easily locate relevant Scriptures for different situations. Read in faith. Remind yourself daily of what God said through the ancient Word.

We must start reminding ourselves of what God said through the Word, because the only thing that will stand as truth is the Word (Psalm 119:160). When our humanity and our human intellect try to get in the way, we must realign with the Word of God. We are encouraged in Jude 1:20 to use our most holy faith to build ourselves up, praying in Holy Spirit. Pray the right answers through divine intelligence. I let the utterings and groanings reset me. They build me up!

In addition to my realignment with the Word, utterings and groanings, and praying in tongues, I incorporate some practical efforts into my practice of leaning on the ancient Word.

First, I write. I write down positive thoughts in a journal. I am known for having multiple journals where I scribble things that will minister to me later. I even use my cell phone's Notes app. And the back of an envelope or a napkin is not off limits if a word of reminder hits my spirit. I believe in writing down words. I have discovered that what you write out you will one day live out. I am a witness of living out the very words I once wrote out. I also put reminders of the words in various places where I can see them often.

Second, I speak life over myself. I affirm myself daily. I remind myself constantly of my purpose and desire to live life abundantly. This is my daily prayer:

Let this mind be in me that's also in Christ Jesus. Lord, teach me Your ways, and help me lean not on my own understanding. Help me to complete the assignment for which You sent me into to earth. Let me be aware of Your presence, and help me be a good steward of Your presence. Let Your will be done; not mine, but Yours.

Third, as a final practical step, I cancel what the enemy is saying with the Word of God—the ancient word *and* prophecies I've received in various ways. I get into worship and meditate on the goodness of God. I take time to reflect on how far God has already brought me, reminding myself if God brought me this far, then He's not done with me yet. I reread all the words that God has sent that prove that the enemy's contradictions are a waste of time because of God's ancient Word that has already gone forth. God's words are the words that will not fail or return to Him void or empty (Isaiah 55:11) but will accomplish what He sent them to do. God's words must see completion—and they will.

Pursuing the Ancient Word of God

The activation of God's Word in our lives comes easily when things are going well. But sometimes the peaks and valleys of life require more than activation. These moments require true discernment and pursuit. I know this to be so because after losing my grandmother and mother back to back, I experienced a spiritual blackout.

Everything was dark—I couldn't hear God, let alone feel or see Him moving. All that I knew about God and everything that I'd been preaching seemed out of reach during that period. It was as if my faith was shaken. Finally Holy Spirit came and sat with me, informing me, *"What you are feeling is your humanity."* And I broke, exposing the fullness of my emotions, and prayed,

Lord, I am disappointed in the outcome of this.

I seized that moment to be completely honest, broken, and vulnerable before the Lord. I kept telling God that I was very disappointed because I had put my trust in Him to heal my mother. However, while tears rolled down my face and I expressed disappointment, the following words came out my mouth with the greatest sense of honesty:

But I trust You even in this.

I began to share with God that I trusted in Him. I said, "Even in a time of disappointment and devastation, I trust

You even in this." As I'm typing these words, and hearing these words again, I still feel such a joy in my heart that I was able to trust God with my innermost feelings. I was vulnerable enough to share my disappointment while still taking Him at His Word and trusting Him in my lowest season. There's a blessing in vulnerability, just like there's a blessing in knowing the Word.

If I'd had less Word in me, that moment of darkness would probably still be overshadowing me to this day. Remember the Word is God, and God is with us even when we walk through the valley of the shadow of death (Psalm 23:4). If you don't have enough Word in you, you will find yourself sinking in a dark hole during valley seasons. But when the Word of God is in us, we have a shield of faith that helps us through trying times. Even if our faith is shook, we can't escape His presence. There's no way around the Word of God. So you might as well go after it.

The more Word you know, the more your faith, your confidence, your hope, and your sense of safety increases. So even when you're praying in tongues, you're going into eternity. You're pulling on what God already said, His ancient Word. When He speaks, we have a due diligence and responsibility to pursue, understand, and mature in His Word. In Luke 2:52 we see that even Jesus grew in wisdom and stature. Jesus had to grow physically and spiritually into a place to carry all of eternity; He had to mature to carry His call.

And if Jesus, being God, matured in that way, then we too have a responsibility to grow in the Word to mature. Even when we don't feel like it, we have to meditate on the Word. Apostle Paul advised believers to "pray without ceasing" (1 Thessalonians 5:17 ESV). Some people think the verse means reciting the same memorized prayer daily. But really, it's about being aware of what you carry, being in constant pursuit of the presence of God, and allowing the Word to become a living epistle (Hebrews 4:12) in your life. It means not limiting prayer to a morning or evening ritual. It means early-bird, lunchtime, and night-owl prayer sessions when Holy Spirit empowers your communion with God. Be ready for Spirit-led prayer anytime and anywhere!

Standing Firm

Some people, including me, stand on business. However, even more than standing on business, I stand firm on the Word of God. We know that grass and everything outside of the Word of God will fail (Isaiah 40:6–8). Therefore, it makes sense to build, believe, and stand on the ancient Word. It was here before us and will remain long after we are gone. As I studied during my mama's health battle, I came across numerous Scriptures, including the ones here, encouraging us to stand firm. Any time the Lord says something, it's important to listen. But when He says it more than once, He really wants us to pay attention to something.

> Therefore, my brothers and sisters, you whom I love and long for, my joy and crown, stand firm in the Lord in this way, dear friends!
>
> Philippians 4:1

> Whatever happens, conduct yourselves in a manner worthy of the gospel of Christ. Then, whether I come and see you or only hear about you in my absence, I will know that you stand firm in the one Spirit, striving together as one for the faith of the gospel.
>
> Philippians 1:27

Be on your guard; stand firm in the faith; be courageous; be strong.

1 Corinthians 16:13

Standing on the Word can prove difficult in a world where people say one thing and do another. I've had my fair share of people not keeping their word to me, and I'm sure you have too. However, dear friend, you can stand on the ancient Word of God. He's different in that He's faithful. And all His words are true. There's no room for error in what He says. You can trust Him. More than that, you can place your hope in Him.

It's okay to have hope. Placing your hope in God comes with a guarantee. You are the living manifestation of an ancient and eternal word. You can trust God because He has already said it, and it's all planned out. You can build your life on His Word because it is a firm foundation to build your life on (Matthew 7:24–27). And in those moments when your emotions try to talk you out of His will and difficulties arise, you can use discernment to pull on His ancient Word as a reminder. In the next chapter we'll dig deeper into what it means when Yahweh remembers us.

PROPHETIC DECREE

I declare you will come into the revelation and awareness of the ancient word declared over your life. May the mysteries of your very breath be unlocked, and may you find rest in knowing that as long as you are breathing, there is still hope unfolding in you. Before God formed you in your mother's womb, He set you apart and sanctified you. God marked you and spoke a word over you. The moment God blew His breath into you, an ancient word was formed. The very breath of God became a word, and God watches over that word to perform it in your life.

The word that you carry can't return to God void and empty, but it will do what it was sent into the earth to do. It won't be done by might, nor by power, but by the Spirit (Zechariah 4:6). The Spirit of God knows the thoughts He has concerning your future, concerning your assignment, and it is the responsibility of Holy Spirit to remind you what God spoke concerning you before time began. You have an ancient word over your life that can't be altered or reversed. Holy Spirit is assigned to ensure that the Word of God is made manifest through you.

I declare you will become everything heaven has declared concerning you. What's inside of you is bigger than you, bigger than your resources, and bigger than your mental and physical capabilities. You don't have the mental space to perceive or fully comprehend what God has set for you. I declare you will hold on to this one thing: All of God's promises for your life are yes and amen. You are moving into a time and season when you must recognize that if it's going to be done, it will be God.

Nothing will be forced. There is nothing you can do to stop, hinder, or help God concerning what He has planned for you. The best thing you can do is pray your future in tongues, allowing Holy Spirit to make intercession for you with groans that are too deep for words. Your future will stand on the shoulders of God.

I declare that everything you do, it will be God. You no longer have to carry the false burden or responsibilities of making it happen. You can't make it happen. You can no longer fight against that word that was declared over you before God wrapped you in flesh and sent you forth into the earth. You don't have to worry about who knows you and who doesn't know you. When heaven has sealed its signature of assignment upon you, no devil in hell can stop the assignment from coming to pass.

God has invested His Word in you, and your destiny will be God. So right now, let go of everything you thought it would take to become; let go of the rejection and pain of being overlooked. Embrace the God-ness of your destiny, and depend on Holy Spirit, who has been sent to lead and guide you into all truth. Acknowledge the Lord in all your ways and watch Him direct your path. Holy Spirit is assigned to ensure that you carry out God's plan for your life. Get ready because it will be God, and Yahweh remembers.

3

YAHWEH REMEMBERS

GOD WILL NOT FORGET!

When I lost my grandmother and mother within months of each other, I thought God had forgotten about me. Yes, the faith-talking, bold-walking Sophia "Comeback Kid" Ruffin herself thought God had forgotten the promises He'd spoken in 2003.

In the place of darkness, I couldn't see how His ancient word was going to show up for me. There was no indication of how all things were working for my good (Romans 8:28). I couldn't find hope, let alone envision my future (Jeremiah 29:11). And I certainly didn't have the strength to pull on God's ancient word for myself. Thankfully, God remembered me (Psalm 136:23). He remembered me, sat with me, and lifted me out of that pit of despair. He even spoke some words to me in that season that I am living today.

Yahweh Remembers

The idea that Yahweh remembers us is one of my favorites on this out-the-blue journey because it's an extension of the ancient word. Sometimes we feel like God must've forgotten about it (insert your own "it" here, because many of us are waiting on something). We experience this feeling of being forgotten because of the delay between prayer and manifestation.

In the waiting period between God's ancient word and our now, what God promised seems like it's being held up. It's taking too long for it to happen. So we think He's forgotten us and our requests. But that couldn't be further from the truth. God sees all and knows all. He will not forget even the one everyone else has written off. He remembers us at our lowest points (Psalm 136:23). He remembers our tears. He remembers our sacrifices when no one was looking. He remembers our press when we felt like giving up.

He's able and most importantly *willing* to meet us there. Right in the place where we've felt left, abandoned, rejected, or overlooked, God will meet us there because He has promises to fulfill. God remembers every word He's ever declared over you, and He watches over them to see their fulfillment in your life (Jeremiah 1:12). We must avoid growing weary and exhausted in the wait (Galatians 6:9).

Fighting Faith Fatigue

Can we be transparent for a moment? Would you agree that sometimes holding on to faith and the promises of God requires more patience and effort than when we're waiting on our family or friends to come through on something? It's like when we can't physically see the thing He's promised, we experience faith fatigue. I describe faith fatigue as that space of tired between your mental exhaustion and your spiritual belief. Your mind and faith feel like they're running on empty as you try to hold on to the Word of God, hold on to the prophecy, and hold on to the promises at the same time. So your everything is tired!

Faith fatigue occurs in those moments when you can't see what you're believing for, but it also seems like the blessing is taking a long time to even hint at an estimated arrival. "Blessing label has been created and is waiting to be received by shipping partner." Sound familiar? The bad news? That's faith fatigue.

But the good news is that Yahweh remembers and at the appointed time He will deliver the promise. We see an example of this with the children of Israel in Exodus 2:23–24 (KJV):

> And it came to pass in process of time, that the king of Egypt died: and the children of Israel sighed by reason of the bondage, and they cried, and their cry came up unto God by reason of the bondage. And God heard their groaning, and God remembered his covenant with Abraham, with Isaac, and with Jacob.

Faith fatigue had really set in for them. But a few things stand out in these verses that give us clarity about how to handle our own faith fatigue. First, we are told that both process and time were required. Nothing was—or is—instant, so we must adjust our expectations to understand that everything requires process and time. Everything comes in due season (Ecclesiastes 3:1). A farmer doesn't plant a seed and expect to see the harvest the same day, yet our microwave mentality has convinced us to have this expectation about God's promises. It's quite the opposite.

Once we receive a promise from the Lord, we are encouraged to wait with expectation and confidence. Psalm 27:14 (AMPC) tells us, "Wait and hope for and expect the Lord; be brave and of good courage and let your heart be stout and enduring. Yes, wait for and hope for and expect the Lord." And we are encouraged to let patience have its perfect work in us, so that once fulfillment comes, we lack nothing (James 1:4).

Second, we are encouraged that even in adverse situations, such as bondage and struggle, we can do something while we wait. When we come up against challenges for which we have no words, we can still express our feelings through cries and groans. The Israelites began to groan, and their groanings connected back to God. Their groans came up as a language that God understood.

I think sometimes we give more credit to people than we do to God. We expect a parent to understand a baby's distinct cries signaling a dirty diaper or empty belly, screams hinting of an ear infection, or groans of stomach discomfort. And we know that parent, moved by their child's needs, will act. Why do we think less of God? Why don't we have faith that He hears our cries, will check on us, *and* will meet our needs?

One thing is certain: I know God hears our groans and stands ready to help us! I know because the Word says, "The righteous cry out, and the LORD hears them; he delivers them from all their troubles" (Psalm 34:17). *The Message* Bible puts it this way: "Is anyone crying for help? GOD is listening, ready to rescue you."

I am proof the ancient Word recorded in Psalm 34:17 still works. After losing the most important women in my life and learning that my groanings can become a part of the delivery of on-target answers, I am even more convinced not to stay silent in my painful places! Your girl Sophia is going to groan. I invite you to join me. Friend, for real: Stop faking it until you make it. Stop pretending to have it all together while falling apart. Claim your deliverance. *Groan!*

Third, Exodus 2:23–24 demonstrates God's remembrance. God remembered His covenant from ancient exchanges. If God did this in the Old Testament, before the Holy Spirit was a constant companion, imagine us crying out to God now with His Spirit *in* us! He is the same yesterday, today, and forever (Hebrews 13:8). God hears us and remembers.

As I think about the losses of my mother and grandmother, there were moments when I thought about the promises that God made to them. Had all of them been fulfilled in their lifetimes? Or were there still some words left for Him to bring to pass? Like my expectation of healing for my mother looked different from what I expected, I realized that how I define fulfillment of a promise can look different from what I expect too. This led me back to the ancient Word. This is what I found:

> Yet the LORD set his affection on your ancestors and loved them, and he chose you, their descendants, above all the nations—as it is today.
>
> Deuteronomy 10:15

> We tell you the good news: What God promised our ancestors he has fulfilled for us, their children, by raising up Jesus. As it is written in the second Psalm: "You are my son; today I have become your father." God raised him from the dead so that he will never be subject to decay. As God has said, "I will give you the holy and sure blessings promised to David."
>
> Acts 13:32–34

> The LORD promised your ancestors Abraham, Isaac, and Jacob that he would give you this land. Now he will take you there and give you large towns, with good buildings that you didn't build.
>
> Deuteronomy 6:10 CEV

> The LORD chose you because he loves you and because he had made a promise to your ancestors. Then with his mighty arm, he rescued you from the king of Egypt, who had made you his slaves.
>
> Deuteronomy 7:8 CEV

I wholeheartedly believe the Lord remembers the prayers of and promises He made with our ancestors and with people who pray for us. And I am absolutely here for an inheritance blessing! That's how I got delivered in the first place. God remembered Doris Ruffin's prayers—and answered them big time. But I believe there may be more in my bloodline that needs redeeming.

What about you? Some of us may need to go back to the family journals and holiday conversations to revisit the promises that God has not forgotten about. "Yahweh remembers" is a clear confirmation that God will not forget you. He knows exactly what He said, and He's going to bring it to pass. God still remembers the covenant, even the one that came before you!

Writing It Down

During a recent flight, I realized the prophetic nature of my travel. I remembered that years ago I had written that I would travel to preach, I would be a wife, and I would prosper in everything I did.

At that time, nothing in my life lined up with any of those things. But if you know me, I'm going to prophesy to myself—believing, speaking, or writing whatever God places on my heart. But to be honest, what I wrote in the journal back then appeared to be impossible dreams and I had no clue how they would become reality. Years later, I'm living out what I wrote out. Just like our spoken words have power, our written words do too. Journaling is more than a notebook and time passing; journals are history books full of God-did-it (and will-do-it) moments. They hint at the jaw-dropping goodness of God's realities for us.

When we go through school, we are taught how to take notes because the notetaking process helps us retain information. Our notetaking does not benefit teachers; they already know the information. We take notes for the present—and future! We take notes to help us prepare for the test. We take notes to retain information.

I take notes with God. I write down the promises He's made to me, through His Word, through prophecies, in our devotion time. If He says something, as I shared in the last chapter, I try to make a note of it somewhere—a journal, a napkin, a cell phone app. Writing it down serves two purposes for me: a reminder of what He said and a receipt—written record—of what He's done. When I am in a place that is testing my faith, I have the reminder of His promises. I can go to His written Word. But the receipts are where the real money resides.

The receipts are proof of my history with God. My history with God has proven that He has come through in every way in my life without failing me. Even through adversity, He's never failed to show up. He's never failed to show me His goodness. And because I have history with Him, I was able to trust Him in what I believe was the biggest loss I've ever experienced in my life.

What about you? Take a moment to think about your history with God. How has God been good to you? How has He exceeded your expectations at times? Don't get in your feelings; check your receipts. I have a feeling God has done more for you than you remember. And I know He has never, ever lied to you (Titus 1:2). Prove me wrong or prove me right—check your receipts.

The receipts we have are for us, not God. But they help us to remain connected and in a trusting relationship with Him. The written records prepare us for the out-of-the-blue experiences. Because we have a relationship, it might look one way, but we're still expecting to see what He told us. We're expecting Him to do a new thing (Isaiah 43:19) that ushers in the jaw-dropping realities of His goodness.

You must remember what He showed you and expect for it to show up that way. Or another way. Either way, *it will be God or it will be God*! "'For my thoughts are not your thoughts, neither are your ways my ways,' declares the LORD" (Isaiah 55:8).

Your written receipt is proof of the promise, like the natural proof of purchase; dig into what you wrote down. Preserve the receipts. Remind yourself often of God's goodness. *I remember that time God did this. I can recall the moment when He showed me that. I have a receipt from that other time when He delivered me from this.* Eventually your time of remembrance will get you through disappointments and setbacks. Writing things down will help you bring what He already remembers to the forefront of your mind. He remembered you before. He'll remember you again. He'll remember you—*always*.

Returning to Remembrance

Even with God's remembrance and our receipts, there are times when our humanity gets the best of us, and our disappointment overrides our faith. When this happens, we respond from our natural understanding and relational habits.

When disappointment and disagreements arise in our human interactions, some of us retreat. Our instinct is to shut down or go mute when we are hurt. Those same interactions typically happen when it comes to being disappointed by God. We withdraw, we disconnect. And sometimes through that disconnection, we fall out of fellowship with the presence of God. It's all because we've been wounded and don't know how to communicate the emotions we're feeling. It doesn't have to be this way.

Zechariah 1:3 reads, "Therefore tell the people: This is what the LORD Almighty says: 'Return to me,' declares the LORD Almighty, 'and I will return to you,' says the LORD

Almighty." The invitation in the ancient Word is available to us. It positions us for living in the jaw-dropping realities of God's goodness. So we don't have to stay disconnected from His presence or His promises.

God is still there waiting for our return. He's cool with us saying, "This hurt me, and I don't know how I'm going to get through it." He can handle us saying, "I apologize for disconnecting," and not hold it against us. God is so good that He's always open for our return. He never reacts, no matter how we cut up.

The Father is always there, open and welcoming, because He remembers His promises concerning you. Your disconnection will not make Him forget what He said about you. Have faith and confidence in knowing Yahweh remembers.

A Word Concerning You

Perhaps you're reading this book and you feel some kind of way because you've lost your strength with what you're facing or what you're dealing with. Maybe it's: "I'm mad at God, I'm hurt, I'm disappointed." "I don't even want to open the Bible and read it." "I don't want to pray" or "I don't know how to pray." If so, I want to challenge you to pray. Talking to God doesn't have to be complicated. No, seriously. Prayer is just a conversation with God, one He's always up for!

And I challenge you to pull on history and the history of your walk with God. Think about how He kept you in the beginning of your walk, the beginning of your journey, and how He has consistently kept you. I challenge you to pull on what you know about God from those historic moments in your personal walk with Him. Pull on your faith and confidence (1 John 5:14) to know if God got you through all of that, even what you didn't understand, then He'll certainly get you through this, whatever your present "this" is. Here's a simple process to get you started:

1. Read Zechariah 1:4. Confess any sin.
2. Acknowledge how you feel at the moment; tell God everything. Be honest. He already knows anyway, but there's something special that happens when you're vulnerable with Him; it leads to intimacy. Relationships deepen with intimacy.
3. Give Him the space and time to respond. Your return to Him and His to you happens through the space of conversation. Remember, it's a relationship.

I believe He has spoken, so there's nothing more for us to do here. He's reminded us that He remembers, so let's take a closer look at the crossroad you may encounter on your journey. Before reading the next chapter, though, take this prophetic decree to heart.

PROPHETIC DECREE

I declare you won't lose hope or fatigue out because of the waiting period of prophetic fulfillment. I declare the gift of faith is being released upon you, and you will rest in knowing that Yahweh remembers.

God has not forgotten the plans that He has for you. For Jeremiah 29:11 (MSG) declares: "I know what I'm doing. I have it all planned out—plans to take care of you, not abandon you, plans to give you the future you hope for." I release this powerful verse over you now.

I declare this will be your security message. This is the very message that secures your future and gives you hope to stand upon.

I declare these will be the days you come into agreement with the word of God for your life and stand on the fact that Yahweh remembers. That He is not man, He can't lie.

God knows the plans He has for you; He created the plans, He wrote them out, and He sent His Spirit to ensure that those plans are executed and carried out. No matter how far away from the plan you get, God has a unique way of bringing you back to His assignment and original intent for your presence in the earth. He remembers what He called you to do. He remembers consecrating you and setting you apart before the foundation of the world. God is mindful of you, and He remembers you.

How could the God of all creation forget you? How could He forget what He sealed you to do? Remember, you didn't choose God, but He chose you. He sanctified you and set you apart. You're a child of God, and He remembers what He said concerning you. His plans for your life are a guarantee, and your future is secured.

Therefore, stand on this: Yahweh remembers exactly what He called you to do. He remembers His covenant He made with your forefathers Abraham, Isaac, and Jacob. He declared a word to Abraham concerning you, and you are the seed of Abraham.

Even as God remembered the children of Israel as they endured oppression and bondage, He remembers you. It was God who heard the groans of the children of Israel during their time of oppression, and He raised up a deliverer. God performed miracles, signs, and wonders as He brought the children of Israel out of bondage. Just as God remembered His covenant then, He remembers it now.

You are not forgotten. Your groan has the power to be heard. For Yahweh makes intercession through you with groanings, and utterances that can't be understood. He understands those wordless words, and when He groans through you, He is responding to the very words He already spoke over you.

I declare when you reach a low place, find yourself at rock bottom, or battle faith fatigue, you will groan. You will rest and allow Holy Spirit to groan through you, articulating supernatural language that has the power to release heaven on earth for you.

4
THE CROSSROAD

HOW MANY TIMES have you heard the stories of the prophet Elijah? Once or more? Never? In either case, Elijah's story provides hope and encouragement for anyone at a crossroad. We see him championing the victories of God throughout the Old Testament. But in the words of Pastor Travis Greene, "You can't just read the Bible, you gotta READ THE BIBLE!"[1] This was the case as I got to 1 Kings 19.

As Elijah was coming off of some really successful victories and the defeat of the false prophets, he was faced with an immediate challenge. Jezebel, a very influential woman, started talking recklessly and threatened the prophet with death: "By this time tomorrow . . ." Her threat scared Elijah and he ran. This victorious prophet didn't just run. He ran into the wilderness (the very place many of us have spent lifetimes trying to leave), sat under a juniper tree, and prayed to die. And as he sat there, he had a choice to make: give up or trust God. Elijah was at the end of himself. He had to shift his focus and trust completely in God.

When you're at a crossroad looking for answers, where do you go? What do you do? You're stuck, unable to make a decision. Like the prophet Elijah, you find yourself "under a juniper tree," afraid to move forward. On one hand you're trying to make it happen with your own strength, and on the other hand you're trying to trust God. You have gone as far as possible on your own, but God sends an answer. How do you respond? With fear or faith?

Everyone always talks about having faith. But what they often fail to mention is that this life of faith is not for the faint of heart. Even as the most victorious of believers we all reach points when we are exhausted. Life gets to lifing, and we, like Elijah, want to say, "I've had enough."

New seasons hit differently. Although we have seen God act on our behalf so many times before, a new season sometimes feels discouraging and overwhelming. We can get so out of breath running from adversity and attacks that we collapse under a tree in the wilderness, saying, "I'm tired. Where You at, God?" We wait on God, wondering when He'll show up—and show out!

That waiting period represents a deciding moment. At that crossroad of decision we are asked to decide between trusting God and remaining stagnant in a place of hiding. We are challenged to shift our focus and trust completely in God, not wavering between two opinions. Am I going to trust what God has said even though what I see is the total opposite? That's when deep faith must kick in, right there at the crossroad. Ask me how I know!

In 2013, I was living in a partially furnished one-bedroom apartment. I would wander between the couch in the front room and the blow-up mattress in the bedroom, my surroundings echoing the extreme lack I was living in. I'd received numerous prophetic words about what my life was going to be like. Every word had something to do with who I was going to become and how God was going to do it. Yet I couldn't see how God was going to make it happen.

One day I lay on the couch in the midst of frustrated petitions, much like Elijah. While lying there, I scrolled through YouTube. I ran into a thumbnail that read "This Year a Prophetic Message for Today." The thumbnail captured my interest because it was a picture of a woman with her head in her lap, slumped over in total exhaustion.

I pressed play and immediately Prophet John Kilpatrick began the prophecy like this:

This year many of you are going to wake up one day and realize you've outgrown where you are. You'll feel like a bird all of a sudden locked up in a cage and you didn't feel that way yesterday, you'll feel desperate to get out and fly to the place that God's prepared for you, and the Lord will open the door.[2]

Something leaped within me. That prophetic word blessed me beyond words. It woke up my hope and faith. I listened to that word multiple times and I began to believe every single word declared. Suddenly, I heard the voice of the Lord say to me, "*It's time to relocate.*"

The voice of the Lord came and confirmed that I would relocate back to Chicago Heights, Illinois, to live with my mama. I was at my own crossroad. I could trust the voice of God from all those prophecies I took to heart, or I could succumb to the perceived embarrassment of moving over four hours to live with my mama again.

You know I immediately started relying on natural understanding rather than spiritual insight, right? My first thoughts: *If You said I'm going to travel, preach, write books, and do all these things, then why am I going back home to live with my mama, Lord? Make it make sense.*

It appeared as if God was preparing to move me *backward*, and not forward. But I was at a crossroad of moving forward or remaining stagnant. The choice was up to me. My future hung on whether I would obey God's guidance.

The power of the crossroad is to unlock your future by an act of obedience. One act of faith will thrust you into prophetic fulfillment! Remember, "faith by itself, if it is not accompanied by action, is dead" (James 2:17). You must act or risk being stuck in a situation that thwarts your purpose and God's plan for your life. What I love is that the Word of God doesn't have to make sense, but He'll still offer us comfort in our vulnerability and uncertainty.

Activating Vulnerability

I believe that Elijah was completely wiped out when he sat under the juniper tree. No matter how prophetically accurate he was, his humanity forced him to a point of vulnerability. The Lord met him there too. We can be strong, prayerful, and faithful and life-altering events will still happen. There will be moments when we want to cry out, "I've had enough." That's a prayer in itself. It's the same one I was praying on my couch that day. It was a prayer of humanity and vulnerability. A prayer of fear and frustration.

What I love most is that the Lord answered Elijah's prayer too. God sent an angel with simple instructions and supernatural provision. "Get up and eat." It was the perfect rescue mission. But it didn't stop there. Elijah lay back down. Can you say tired?

I've been there, so worn-out by circumstances that I only had enough physical strength to enjoy the small, answered prayer of God. And unable to see beyond that moment, pick myself up, and move forward. The angel came back to Elijah and said, "Get up and eat, for the journey is too much for you" (1 Kings 19:7).

When you're stuck under a juniper tree of your choosing, how do you respond to God's provision? Being at the low point of struggle is the very place to lean into vulnerability—and authenticity, especially in prayer. But sometimes we make prayer a chore or mimic how other people pray, thinking we sound more holy or deep. Other times, we pray like we have an expectation of how we think a situation should go.

Sure, those prayers reach God. Yet God welcomes, hears, and answers our "end of rope" prayers too. He answers our vulnerable, open, and raw outcries.

Personally, my greatest results in prayer have been when I've been vulnerable and honest with God. When I've cried out real (and sometimes ugly), I've received real answers. His gentleness responded just like it did for Elijah. No wind. No earthquake. No fire. Just a still, small voice. *Gentleness.*

God's gentleness is indescribable; nothing in our human experience equals it. He responds to our human expression of raw outcries with gentleness. That's just how great of a Father God is. He's not into matching energy. He's into responding from the place of relationship. Our calling out in deep emotion does not negate our relationship. Instead, our vulnerability unlocks a new level of personal relationship with God. And we get closer to living in the jaw-dropping realities of God's goodness.

What have you been holding in? You know the thing that rolls around in your mind when you pull into the garage and just sit for a moment because life feels heavy—that thing. That articulation of exasperation is exactly what Holy Spirit is present for. He's communicating those sighs, silent tears, and rageful screams into something Father God both understands and responds to. Our prayer becomes most powerful when we're honest with ourselves and God. God is moved by our honesty and true relationship, not our religion. His presence shows up, releasing breakthrough.

Stop Wavering and Make a Decision

My friend, there comes a time in every believer's journey when we come to the end of ourselves. We find ourselves at the low point of a struggle, faced with a decision: stay stuck or trust God. This crossroad is where many of us get stuck wavering between two opinions. Staying at the crossroad too long allows our mind and humanity to talk us out of obeying God. We begin thinking about how it's going to work and start trying to make something happen in our own strength. At that point, we're no longer following God. We're following our own strength, intellect, and—oftentimes—emotions.

Think about it: God has already given you instructions or a promise. It didn't make sense when He said it, but you got excited and claimed the word anyway. You latched on to the promise that was intellectually impossible by trusting in His ancient Word:

> But God hath chosen the *foolish* things of the world to *confound the wise*; and God hath chosen the weak things of the world to confound the things which are mighty.
>
> 1 Corinthians 1:27 KJV, emphasis added

Then you got tired of picking it up and looking at it, trying to figure out how it was going to work out. No matter how long you stare at a situation, it's never going to make sense, especially if you're looking at it with your own wisdom. God's wisdom is far greater than ours. He sees way ahead. While our limited mind can see the forest *or* the trees, God's infinite creativity made the forest *and* the trees. He knows it all and holds it all. Our job is to make the decision of faith to believe the originator of the promise.

And our job is to *not* waver between two opinions. When wavering between two opinions, we allow doubt to take root. The apostle James wrote about doubt, especially as it relates to prayer. He warned, "Anyone who doubts is like a wave in the sea, blown up and down by the wind. Such doubters are thinking two different things at the same time, and they cannot decide about anything they do. They should not think they will receive anything from the Lord" (James 1:6–8 NCV).

The good news is you can stop wavering and trust God to provide direction. That's exactly what I did when I made the decision October 31, 2013, to relocate from Mount Vernon, Illinois, to Chicago Heights to live with my mother. I made the decision to trust God even when it didn't make sense.

As I followed God's instruction, *He* led me every step of the way, meeting me with favor after favor. I was able to end my lease agreement early without penalty; I quit my job, packed up my clothes, and set out on the journey of a new beginning. I moved back home with my mother. During that time frame God began to transform my ministry. I went from local to global in a matter of three years post-transition. God platformed my ministry from a social media app called Periscope, which allowed users to stream live videos and connect with viewers around the world. I met Apostle John Eckhardt, and he endorsed my ministry, showed me favor, and opened many doors for me.

One act of obedience in 2013 unlocked new seasons in my life. And my obedience to go live on Periscope opened doors of ministry that perhaps would not be opened to me today. No, really! See, Periscope was only in operation for roughly six years—just long enough for God to use it for His glory as a transformational tool in my life and ministry.

Friend, take note: Move when God says move. His open door may not stay open forever! But don't move with fear. Boldly step out in faith. The crossroad requires faith to believe God and trust the process. That one move to my mama's house unlocked books, relationships, and favor, and an influx of new.

Follow the GPS

God's ancient Word is a navigation system for our future. We can rely on it every day—and more than any natural GPS we use daily. I rarely go anywhere without using my car's GPS, especially since moving to a new city. I'm always amazed when I find myself going someplace I've gone several times before but still turning on my navigation system. I have come to rely on that voice guiding me to my destination, trusting that it is going to take me the safest, fastest way.

The Word of God is our spiritual GPS. When we obey it, we can trust that we will safely get to the place that God has for us and avoid unnecessary delays.

Accessing God's Word as a navigation system requires discernment, trust, and knowledge of God. Like in the natural when we respond easily to a GPS's varying instructions, spiritually we have to become comfortable with easily following God's instructions. We also must trust God's Word, especially when it's taking us in an *unknown direction* to a place we've been to many times before. Have you ever over-ridden the GPS's direction because you knew a better way, only to find yourself stuck in heavy traffic? You only have to do that once before thinking twice about making the same mistake.

Friend, don't pay more attention to your GPS than to God's Word. His Word actively helps us bypass unseen obstructions and unnecessary delays. His ways are not our ways; His heavenly viewpoint is higher than ours (Isaiah 55:8–9). We must discern when we are getting distracted or in our own way.

While we're talking about the navigation experience, have you ever tried to race or beat your GPS's estimated time of arrival? That effort may give us an adrenaline rush, but it's usually a waste of time. Sometimes that's how we are with God's Word. We try to rush it. How's that worked for you? It hasn't for me! I've learned that we can't rush God—ever. Instead, we must trust that He's going to get us where we are supposed to be at the perfect time.

Habakkuk 2:3 reminds us, "For the revelation awaits an appointed time; it speaks of the end and will not prove false. Though it linger, wait for it; it will certainly come and will not delay." Stop trying to rush God's timing. Remember, rushing, whether spiritually or naturally, has pitfalls. Not to be scary, but just realistic, it's important to remember there is danger in rushing through the crossroad—collisions happen. It's okay to slow down. God's GPS has taken the speed limit into account when calculating your proper arrival time.

A final component of following God's Word as a navigation system is knowing Him. Having a relationship with God helps with resting in the knowing. Knowing God well means you know that His Holy Spirit will lead you. If you acknowledge Him in all your ways, He'll make your path straight. That's a promise straight out of Proverbs 3:6. We can trust it too. On God's straight path we won't weave in and out of purpose and get carsick on the way to God's next!

But we have to know Him well enough to bring Him into a situation. We have to be honest. We have to be vulnerable. "Lord, I'm afraid. I don't know all the turns ahead, *but* I trust You." This level of trust is faith, and faith requires relationship. Again, navigating the crossroad is all about deeper faith and greater intimacy. It gets easier navigating crossroads the more you take faith moves in relationship with God, and act on His instructions. You begin to move off your history with God. Our history increases our faith to believe in Him because He's always shown up. We can take God at His Word.

Rerouting and Holding Patterns

While we're talking about travel, it's important to acknowledge the possibilities of rerouting and holding patterns. My itinerary keeps me traveling three to four times per week. As a result of a few frustrating experiences, I've learned to build in additional travel time for required rerouting and holding patterns.

Rerouting happens most often when there is a delay ahead of us that will alter our expected arrival time. The route will change, sometimes taking a more scenic or residential route to our destination. Many times, even with a rerouting experience, we still arrive close to our originally expected time. I'm cool with a reroute that keeps me from sitting in my car in stagnant highway traffic.

However, in-flight holding patterns put me on edge. I'm looking out the window, seeing the city, and knowing that we can't land there. We're circling above where we're supposed to be but just can't quite take possession of the landing space. As with airplanes, life's holding patterns put us in a wait that can cause anxiety. We begin to feel pressure and a deep desire for a *now* landing. In the air and in life, I go to Romans 8:26–28 (MSG). It reads like this:

> Meanwhile, the moment we get tired in the waiting, God's Spirit is right alongside helping us along. If we don't know how or what to pray, it doesn't matter. He does our praying in and for us, making prayer out of our wordless sighs, our aching groans. He knows us far better than we know ourselves, knows our pregnant condition, and keeps us present before God. That's why we can be so sure that every detail in our lives of love for God is worked into something good.

It can be uncomfortable when a person gets to the phase when they're waiting on God for something positive while simultaneously dealing with something negative. This happens because the longer you wait, the more you're being enlarged in the waiting. During pregnancy, for example, a mother's womb enlarges to accommodate a growing baby. As she waits on her due date, the more uncomfortable she gets.

You are growing up spiritually. Expect to be enlarged! Enlargement is a good thing. If you're like me when I stumbled upon my crossroad, you'll need to grow up spiritually before receiving what God has planned for you. So don't quit! Sometimes people get tired and give up while waiting, causing premature or unsafe experiences. Trust that in the wait, no matter how long it takes, the rerouting or holding pattern is for your good.

When God told me to go back to my mama's house, I felt like I was being punished. I believed that by moving in with her I'd be going backward instead of forward. I'd be starting completely over, needing a new job and everything. I could decide to stay where I was—robbing Peter to pay Paul—in the dysfunctional pattern of lack. Or I could reroute and go back home. That was a pivotal crossroad. I weighed the pros and cons, hoping to be practical. "Okay, which scenario makes sense?" The best decision that makes sense is to obey God.

I chose to reroute and go back home. That decision turned out to be preparation for living in the jaw-dropping realities of God's goodness. I didn't know it then, but any act of faith founded on obedience is a step forward. That's true even when it feels like we've lost momentum.

Going backward or experiencing a holding pattern is usually an indication that God is about to catapult you. Obedience is always connected to a catapult. Either we're going to sit, remain the same, and complain, or we're going to decide to act on the instructions God's already given—reroute or hang tight in a holding pattern until cleared for landing.

I believe the crossroads prepare us for a shift in our trajectory. However, the timing of the shift is dependent on how long we wait on obeying God. You can delay what God wants to do by your disobedience. Delayed obedience is challenging because it can cause you to miss the window of landing or opportunity. If I had delayed jumping on Periscope and had not consistently uploaded encouraging prophetic content, who knows where I'd be today. It's possible that you wouldn't be reading this book because I may have been *still* inconsolably wandering in the valley of the shadow of death, never entering my *it will be God or it will be God* season.

Yes, obeying God during life's rerouting or holding patterns is really that serious. And I understand if that fact is difficult to grasp right now. Choosing to obediently accept the rerouting or holding pattern at a crossroad requires a mindset shift. Ultimately, we must stand on what God said is so. His plan is to fulfill the promise. If God be God, serve Him.

If God Be God

Mindset matters. That's what we learn when we check back in with Elijah at his crossroad. "Elijah went before the people and said, 'How long will you waver between two opinions? If the LORD is God, follow him; but if Baal is God, follow him.' But the people said nothing" (1 Kings 18:21). Every time I read or hear this Scripture I am struck by how people said nothing. They had to be just out of their minds for there to be any comparison. But as I think about it more, I realize how likely it was that they were simply confused. That's what wavering does; it causes us to be confused. It's likely their confusion, coupled with their conditioning and lived experiences, prevented them from fully committing to follow God.

Like the Israelites, we're not immune to confusion. However, we can adopt an "if God be God" mindset to silence the chatter of confusion that causes us to freeze at the crossroad.

Adopting an "if God be God" mindset is rooted in our history with God. Looking back on the things, great and small, that God has done for us builds our faith. Even when we didn't know any better in some areas, God was still gracious and merciful toward us.

I used to think it was only the old people who'd say things like "When I look back over my life" and "If it had not been for the Lord on my side." I was wrong! Those are the refrains of people who are pulling on their history with God. We can look at how far God has brought us, including the distance and deliverance from the times when we didn't even fully know Him.

As long as you have a memory to pull on, you have something to help you navigate the crossroad. He did this before; imagine what He'll do now or next. The secret is pulling on what He's already done: God did this!

Pulling on your history with Him helps you continuously develop a relationship of trust. It's the same as with your parents, friends, or spouse—your trust is based on experience, how they've been there for you in the past. They showed up, and now you consider them dependable and trustworthy. If you hit a crisis, you know whom to call. If this happens in a personal relationship with people, imagine taking this mindset and applying it to your relationship with God. It will revolutionize your faith, preparing you for life in the jaw-dropping goodness of God's realities. Your relationship with Him delivers closeness. The trust and intimacy you build with Him allows you to take a courageous, confident stance at a crossroad—I trust God. *It will be God or it will be God* because God always works it out.

That crossroad represents your defining decision moment. You have gone as far as you can on your own, and now it's time to make a choice. Will God be God or will you choose an alternative source or path of provision or deliverance? Choose God! Although it may not seem like it, God sends answers at the crossroad. Isaiah 30:21 tells us, "Whether you turn to the right or to the left, your ears will hear a voice behind you, saying, 'This is the way; walk in it.'"

Let me be transparent: Making the choice to walk will be easier said than done. We will have to walk in some dark places, which I'll discuss in the next chapter. But have faith! We have God's history to pull on and His ancient Word as a lamp to our feet and light to our paths (Psalm 119:105).

PROPHETIC DECREE

Get ready to cross over into the land of milk and honey. For the breaker has already gone before you. He has made your crooked places straight. Take the leap of faith, and cross over. Even when you find yourself hitting rock bottom, stuck in between a rock and a hard place, arise and shine for your light has come and the glory of the Lord is upon you. Even as the Lord declared to Elijah, "Arise and eat for the journey is too great for you."

I declare unto you, Arise, and get in your Word, for there is a great journey ahead of you.

I declare supernatural ravens will bring you a divine provision that will cause you to arise and live. So I say unto you: Arise, arise, arise. It's time to cross over. There is so much purpose in you on the other side of where you are now. Don't you dare allow fear of failure, defeat, or anxiety to hinder you from crossing over.

I declare the Spirit of God is moving upon you now, and every demonic web you've been entangled in is losing its grip.

I declare as you cross over and obey you will walk into an Ephesians 3:20 season. A season that goes above your imagination and beyond your ability to even dare to ask or think according to the power that is already working within you. For you already have access to the power to do it, and you have the resource within you and possess everything you need to accomplish everything heaven has ordained and endorsed for you to do.

You have exactly what it takes. You have been equipped with the power and authority to get the job done. Heaven is with you for you to embody the headquarters of heaven within you; therefore, arise and shine for your light has come, and the glory of the Lord is upon you. You will enter a time of the unthinkable happening for you. You will run into new doors, new opportunities, new miracles, new promotions, new breakthroughs, and new favor. They will be above what you could have ever dreamed.

I declare these will be the days when before you even think it, the manifestation will knock at your door. Imagine receiving what you have yet to pray for.

I declare this dimension over each of you, that you will experience a time and season of the unimaginable. I say unto you: Cross over.

5

THE DARK BEFORE
THE DAWN

WHEN DARKNESS STORMED IN as I contemplated my mother's illness, I was overwhelmed by its ferocity and strength. It attacked my senses, temporarily shutting down acute awareness of things around me. All sound ceased. All vision disappeared. All that I was was plunged into the unknown. I fought darkness for what seemed like forever. In reality, it was just about three months.

After more than ninety days at my mother's hospital bedside, my family and I made an agonizing decision. We based our decision off the expectation of healing. And so it was that my mother was healed. She transitioned from this earth into God's kingdom. Suddenly, she was healed! But I want to dig a bit deeper into what really happens in the darkness.

I shared in the introduction that the darkness was when God downloaded to me the *it will be God or it will be God* message that you're taking in right now. But it was more than *just* a message. What I really experienced in that darkness was a supernatural reset.

For generations many of us have been taught to fear the dark. We inch toward darkness with shaking uncertainty— stretched hands feeling for what's around us, dragged feet creeping into the unknown, squinted eyes hoping to adjust. Sudden descents into darkness cause us to panic— contemplating how long it will last, wondering if other people are experiencing the same thing, mind racing to the worst.

But what if we began to face darkness with a different posture?

When the blackout happens, we can simply stand still. Standing still allows us to take deep breaths, clear our minds, and choose wisdom. According to astronomers, the darkest part of the night is when there is no sunrise or sunset and the sun is farthest below the horizon. Even as it is dark, it is not long before the sun breaks forth and light returns.

Supernatural Reset

When life gets so overwhelming and you can no longer see, stand still. The light will return. God is about to change the scene of your life and instigate a supernatural reset. In the natural world, phones and devices can be restored to the manufacturer's settings with what's known as a hard reset. I describe supernatural resets as a restoration to the heavenly settings—on earth as it is in heaven (Matthew 6:10).

The moment darkness arrives and you're not sure if you're coming, going, or even going to get through, don't panic. A supernatural reset is on the way. Bear with me as I return to the electronic device analogy. Some devices emit a sound when powering down. In our case that sound is often a groan, maybe a roar as the last amount of our natural power exits our body. It's the moment when you hit rock bottom and your own wailing may sound so distant or foreign that you don't even recognize that it's you who's crying out. That's when Holy Spirit's power is activated to come in and help you. He begins to intercede as described in Romans 8:26–27:

> In the same way, the Spirit helps us in our weakness. We do not know what we ought to pray for, but the Spirit himself intercedes for us through wordless groans. And he who searches our hearts knows the mind of the Spirit, because the Spirit intercedes for God's people in accordance with the will of God.

Some of us can think of times when our grandmothers, mothers, or church elders interceded for us. Their intensity shook rooms and caused pounding on altar steps. Mattress sides and pews creaked under the weight of their determination to see breakthrough on behalf of someone else. Carpets bore imprints of their prone posture as they wept and moaned for the salvation and deliverance of loved ones.

We knew a change was coming when Mother So-and-So prayed. I imagine Holy Spirit interceding for us with even greater intensity. We can rest assured that when we are in the darkness, Holy Spirit's prayers will literally shake heaven and release an outpouring. Supernatural reset is initiated when Holy Spirit steps in, interceding. But our obedience will be a determining factor in whether we fully experience that reset.

Reset Requires Obedience

In the first chapter of Ruth we see three women—Naomi, Orpah, and Ruth—enter a dark season. Their husbands died. Famine reigned in the land. The three women lost everything. They had to leave where they were. A greater decision had to be made: stay together in the uncertainty or go their separate ways in hopes of finding restoration. I believe Orpah and Ruth both made the best decision for themselves at that crossroad.

However, I believe that Ruth's obedience to staying with Naomi caused her to experience a supernatural reset, not just for herself but for Naomi too. Ruth was obeying God's will even without realizing it at the time. Have you ever been there? Made a decision and later realized God was in it? That's basically what Ruth—and Naomi—did. Their decision at a dark crossroad allowed them to experience restoration, even after great loss.

When looking at restoration, we think of God replacing what we lost. At the surface level, it may not be exactly what it was before. Yet it will be exactly what is needed for our next. It appeared as if Ruth and Naomi had both lost everything—their husbands and provision. However, their relationship of trust and obedience set them up for a total reset. In Ruth chapter four we see the full outcome of their obedience. Ruth found a husband *and* birthed a son. Naomi received an extended legacy. They both experienced abundance and multiplication. Women said the following to Naomi about her grandson:

> He will renew your life and sustain you in your old age. For your daughter-in-law, who loves you and who is better to you than seven sons, has given him birth.
>
> Ruth 4:15

Resets bring restoration! Restoration is God multiplying your life. The Lord will go before you. The righteousness of God will go ahead of you. Those who walked in darkness will see a great light, and God in His goodness, His glory, and His righteousness will go before you. One season will feel like a loss, while the next will feel like multiplication. The only requirement is our obedience.

Our dark seasons give us a chance to choose obedience.

Upon choosing obedience we experience the ancient Word of God in simple yet magnificent ways. We experience the joy of the Lord transforming into our strength as described in Nehemiah 8:10: "Nehemiah said, 'Go and enjoy choice food and sweet drinks, and send some to those who have nothing prepared. This day is holy to our Lord. Do not grieve, for the joy of the LORD is your strength.'" After obedience, joy is inexplicable. It surpasses all understanding—just like the peace mentioned in Philippians 4:7.

Can we pause right here for a second? There have been times when I have quoted "peace that passes" all understanding. But as I was preparing this section, I was drawn to the specificity of *surpasses* in the Scripture. *Pass* simply means to move past something, while *surpasses* refers to moving beyond in quality or expected experience. Other words for *surpass* include *exceed*, *outdo*, and *excel*.

I don't want us to merely want to pass the dark place with some joy. I want the joy on the other side of our darkness to exceed our expectations! Do you feel me? Good. Now we can get back into the other blessings of obedience in the reset.

Like Ruth, we make room for life again through our obedience to the will of God. God will revive or replace things that were dead. Our obedience through the reset brings life in new ways. And that happens in such ways that only God can get the glory.

Breaking of Day

After we've come through our darkness, many people will wonder, "Where did your joy come from?" "How did you arrive at such a place of peace so quickly?" The truthful answer will be that it was a supernatural reset. Only God can hit the reset button, delivering such strength and an abundance of joy. God's ancient word is the only force powerful enough to flip our testimony in such grand ways.

When God sends a "let there be light" word into your darkness, supernatural light is separated from darkness, and He calls it good (Genesis 1:3). As a result, your relationship with Him will go to another level. He will show up in places and spaces where no one else can. We see confirmation of His light entering in in several places from the onset of creation.

According to author Lisa Loraine Baker, darkness and night are referenced almost 150 times in the Bible, while light appears nearly double that. We see *day* written more than 1,600 times.[1] That's ten times more mentions of light, reminding us that darkness cannot remain forever! Because my ultimate goal throughout this book is to strengthen your faith, I think it's important to share some of these verses with you:

Do not gloat over me, my enemy! Though I have fallen, I will rise. Though I sit in darkness, the LORD will be my light.

Micah 7:8

But you are a chosen people, a royal priesthood, a holy nation, God's special possession, that you may declare the praises of him who called you out of darkness into his wonderful light.

1 Peter 2:9

The light shines in the darkness, and the darkness has not overcome it.

John 1:5

Then your light will break forth like the dawn, and your healing will quickly appear; then your righteousness will go before you, and the glory of the LORD will be your rear guard.

Isaiah 58:8

I saved Isaiah 58:8 for last because it's one of my favorites. Of the promises found in the ancient Word, this Scripture is so good because it lists multiple promises. First, God promises breakthrough light. That means no matter what the darkness holds or how long it lasts, light has to come. Second, He promises healing will come, and quickly at that. Your season of darkness may last what feels like ten days or ten years, but your healing is coming swiftly! I'm going to share about the suddenly a little later, but you can shout right here for now.

The third promise mentioned in Isaiah 58:8 is that righteousness will go before you. That means God's way and principles will go ahead of you. Those who walked in darkness will see the light of God (Isaiah 9:2). His goodness and His glory will go before you, preparing a way of peace. The ancient Word confirms that the glory of the Lord will be your rear guard.

Having the glory of the Lord guarding your back is something else. Think about it like this: You know your best friend, cousin, or spouse has got your back. They're coming behind you, ready for all the smoke. Just think about what it means to have God's literal glory having your back. Your mama having your back ain't got nothing on God having your back!

Being on guard means being on defense, prepared for any enemy attack or advancement that might come. Whether in sports, the military, cybersecurity, or any other context, guards must be alert and watchful. God's glory on guard? Impenetrable! Whatever's happening in your darkness, just hold on because His glory must break forth like the dawn in your life.

There's Glory After This

In 2021, I hosted the After This Glory Conference in Chicago, Illinois. During one of the sessions about twenty women came up and shared their testimonies of glory after their darkness. Worshiper Jenny Weaver tapped in to include her testimony of transformation from being a witch and a con woman. She shared openly about how she'd been on the streets, depressed and suicidal. And now she's leading prophetic worship and deliverance services globally! Jenny found glory after all that she'd been through. Your season of darkness may not be the same as Jenny's, but God's glory that she's experiencing is the same.

No matter how deep or dark a season is, God offers us a reminder in Romans 8:18 that there will be glory on the other side. I love how the New Living Translation lays it out: "Yet what we suffer now is *nothing* compared to the glory *he* will reveal to us later" (emphasis added).

The Hebrew word for glory is *kabob*, meaning "weight and significance." When we break this Scripture down, we see that after all of our experiences God Himself will reveal weight and significance in our lives. He'll deliver luxury, grandeur, or magnificence, and I'm not talking about material possessions either. I'm talking about experiencing luxurious rest as a result of peace. I'm referencing how grand life feels when we are no longer burdened by insignificant distractions. Can you imagine the magnificence of deeper relational intimacy with God and our loved ones? These benefits are the weight of His glory!

> For this light momentary affliction is preparing for us an eternal weight of glory beyond all comparison, as we look not to the things that are seen but to the things that are unseen. For the things that are seen are transient, but the things that are unseen are eternal.
>
> 2 Corinthians 4:17–18 ESV

As we continue with this "after this" glory party, it is important to note that carrying weight requires capacity. Capacity is the maximum amount that something can contain. Weight lifters, for example, train to increase their capacity for lifting. Let's bring it closer to home. Most of us shift the way we carry water and goods to extend our carrying capacity. You and I both load up those grocery bags, trying to limit the number of times we have to go back and forth between the car and the kitchen. Fingers, hands, and forearms just straining!

So what happens when we reframe the experience of our dark seasons? What if God is just helping us to max out our capacity?

God won't put more on you than you can bear. I know that phrase isn't Scripture. It often seems like a cliché when people say it. But in dark seasons, you may discover a greater capacity to bear more stuff because God is really doing the heavy lifting! You may also discover that what you're feeling isn't always warfare; it's capacity building, weight lifting.

You're being stretched to go from glory to glory (2 Corinthians 3:18), so you have to have capacity to carry the weight. You're going from weight to weight. From luxury to luxury! Your present season can't be compared to what's next because it's going to make God known! Like the heavens declaring the glory of God (Psalm 19:1), your new season will have power to speak without making a sound or a word. The message will go forth through you, putting God's glory on display.

The skies display God's craftmanship and artistry. We are His handiwork (Ephesians 2:10). When we overcome challenges or survive what should have killed us, we are displaying God's handiwork. Our lives are evidence of His artistry and mastery. His glory after this, whatever our "this" is, is part of His workmanship; it all adds to the wonderful complexity of how we are made (Psalm 139:14).

This present darkness is not a period. It is a semicolon, a pause, in your life. You have the capacity to carry eternal glory! A plan is being released to allow you to experience the glory of God. As this dark season passes, I declare that you will have a cool-of-the-day encounter with God (Genesis

3:8) without having to hide! After this you will display God's artistry in full splendor without shame.

Whatever you are enduring in this season, you will not break. Whatever the journey is that you're up against, you will not break. Whatever mountain you're facing must come down. The giant attempting to rob you of your joy, peace, and focus will not break you. I prophesy that you will not break. There will be glory after this.

I can declare this over your life with such confidence because of how I've experienced it in my own life. In my darkest hour, God gave me hope. Truly it was an overflow of hope because I'm still clinging to it and have enough to share with you.

The supernatural reset that I shared with you earlier repositions us. Reset positions us for an upgrade to the glory of God. The glory acting as your rear guard in a dark place becomes the glory that shines upon you, offering a new outlook and peace (Numbers 6:24–25) when your position changes. The sun is always shining, but earth's position determines where it faces.

God's glory is always present; how it manifests is based on your position. Isaiah 60:1 says it like this: "Arise, shine, for your light has come, and the glory of the LORD rises upon you." That means your position must change, you've got to get up. Can I keep it one hundred with you, though? Getting up when it's dark is hard!

I remember saying to God during my dark season, "I don't want the anointing, or oil, that comes with this season of crushing." I didn't want any oil from the loss of my mother. Yet I kept feeling God supernaturally pouring into my life the more broken I became. And the Lord kept telling me that my crushing was producing fresh oil. God's glory and anointing on my life increased in that season, and it didn't seem fair.

I felt like I was at rock bottom, stuck in darkness; however, I couldn't go any lower. At the lowest moment in life, the only source of hope is calling on Jesus. In that place of desperation and in the midst of my dark season, I knew I needed God. When I cried out, He heard me, He answered me, and most of all He lifted me out of darkness with His marvelous light.

I needed to be closer to God and His presence. I could continue trying to stare into the darkness and make sense of what I was seeing. Or I could turn my face to His glory. I love God so much because He stayed with me. Even in the darkness, His presence was there, waiting on me to draw near to Him. And as I drew near to Him, James 4:8 became a reality. God came close to me just as the verse promised. The heart work happened. I was able to focus, and I found peace in the presence of the Lord.

Dark seasons are no joke—and the related pressure isn't either! But my experience reminds me of how gemstones are created. I recently learned that gemstones, not just diamonds, are created through various pressure and conditioning moments. Rubies are created under extreme pressure and heat deep in the earth. And if certain elements are introduced during the process, the ruby can become pink or even orange. Another plot twist came when I learned that sapphires and rubies are the same mineral that experienced different conditions.[2]

Now, get this: The size of these beautiful stones is determined by how quickly they cool. Fast cooling yields a small stone. Slow cooling allows for the stones to grow larger.[3] I don't know about you, but I like a bit of bling. If you follow me on social media, you've seen the drip—even my water bottle has a little charm!

The information on gemstones really helped me to understand how my anointing grew as I went through dark pressure.

I'm not promoting suffering, but I am encouraging you not to be surprised when growth occurs even in your deepest dark places. And don't be surprised by your new intimacy with God. The Bible declares, "If we suffer, we shall also reign with him" (2 Timothy 2:12 KJV).

Friend, you may be facing your largest battle to date and feel like everything has gone dark on you. The pressure may be an intensity you've never experienced before. You know that nobody can get you out of this but God. I want to encourage you to draw near to Him, even in this. He's going to reach for you as you reach for Him. He's going to show up and shine the light of glory into your situation. No matter what it looks like, He's going to step in. He's going to work behind the scenes of your life to position you for His jaw-dropping goodness.

Have you ever been to a play or performance in a theater? At certain points during the production things go completely dark. In some cases, the curtains close altogether. When the lights come back on there's an entirely new scene before you on the stage. You didn't see the people moving all the props around. You couldn't see the performers changing costumes, but change happened.

That's what the seasons of darkness remind me of, a set change. God is working behind the scenes to cover you. He's hiding you until the perfect time for the lights to come back on. He's hiding us; we just have to be willing to dwell in that shadowy space when it comes. He loves us so much that He'll never leave us behind or desolate. We just have to learn to rest until the glory comes. His ancient Word promises, "Whoever dwells in the shelter of the Most High will rest in the shadow of the Almighty" (Psalm 91:1).

Shadows can't happen without light!

Before you know it, you'll wake up and realize you've got full light, life, and strength. The entire scene in your life will have changed. When the scene changes and light shines, you may find yourself a little disoriented like you do when you're stepping out of a dark theater. That's okay because Holy Spirit will be there to help you. We'll get into accessing the Helper in the next chapter.

PROPHETIC DECREE

I declare, "God is bringing you back to the original intent for which you were sent into the earth, the original reason you were formed."

I declare that the chaos you are experiencing will cause the light of God's glory and goodness to be released upon you. You may not be able to see now, you may not be able to fully understand this season, but I declare unto you this season will cause the light of God to shine out of darkness.

I declare you are waking up and coming into the reality that there is no other God, or no other name above His name. Everything you've depended upon as your god, or as your idol, has forsaken you, and the only name you are able to call upon is the name of Jesus. I declare God is making His name strong and watching over His word to perform it in your life.

I say unto you, Lazarus, awaken. Your situation will not bury you alive. You will not smell like death. I command you to take off those graveclothes, remove the odor of destiny death. And I command resurrecting power to come forth. These are the days you shall live and not die. The dream in you can't die, the purpose in you can't die, the assignment in you can't die. The enemy is upon the earth, but the Spirit of God declares, "Live." Just as the death angel passed by the blood, He is passing by the blood even now. You have purpose, and an assignment to fulfill.

Just as God ordained John to be sent into the earth, so has He ordained you. Before John was born, the prophet Isaiah declared in Isaiah 40:3 (NLT), "Listen! It's the voice of someone shouting, 'Clear the way through the wilderness for the LORD! Make a straight highway through the wasteland for our God!'" John's assignment was determined before he made his entrance into the earth. Each time John was challenged on his identity and his purpose, he declared, "I am a voice shouting in the wilderness, 'Clear the way for the Lord's coming.'" Even as John knew and recognized his original intent in the earth, so shall you.

Your original intent is to love the Lord your God with all of your heart, mind, and soul. To be intimate with Holy Spirit and entrust Holy Spirit to lead you and guide you into all truth. For it is Holy Spirit who knows the very thoughts of God concerning you. These are the days you will get back to the place of original intent. The real reason you were sent into the earth.

6

ACCESS THE HELPER

WHEN I GAVE MY LIFE TO GOD, people gave me anxiety! Family members and leaders in the church shared their opinions about my spiritual progress. I should have been at a certain point in my walk with God by a certain time. Their well-meaning attempts to put me and God in a box together with a timetable for when I'd pop out whole was not effective. Friend, they had me in a religious chokehold!

Instead of enjoying my new walk with God, I started to panic and tried to do things that would please people, which created a mess down the road. Their hope for my discipleship began to hold me hostage; I was focused more on man than on God. Looking back, and as I journey with others, I have come to realize that a more effective strategy is to encourage believers to seek ways to know and access Holy Spirit as their helper.

Right now, there is a fight for your future as you enter seasons that you've never been in before. Seasons that position you for the jaw-dropping realities of God's goodness. You may not know what to do or where to turn, but God has promised us, in His ancient Word, access to a helper. Jesus promised the disciples, "I will ask the Father, and he will give you another advocate to help you and be with you forever—the Spirit of truth. The world cannot accept him, because it neither sees him nor knows him. But you know him, for he lives with you and will be in you" (John 14:16–17). You may not know exactly what you need or how to get it, but there's an advocate working on your behalf.

As a former social worker, I know how important it is to have someone advocate for our best interests. Social workers are tasked with being advocates for others. This means that they are responsible for speaking on behalf of someone. Social workers work to ensure clients' rights are being received and applied appropriately. As advocates, they identify instances of discrimination and unfairness. They also fight for benefits, access, and provision.

Social workers are liaisons, speaking up for their clients and representing their interests with other parties. They have access to lawyers, therapists, and judges, all key decision makers regarding clients' cases. Similarly, Holy Spirit takes on this role for us in the spirit realm. When we don't know what to ask for or how to get it, the Holy Spirit is available to advocate for us. He can act on our behalf, representing us to make sure that we are receiving what we need.

The key to unlocking the mysteries of heaven concerning how to navigate any season comes from Holy Spirit. Because of this, I want to make sure that as you continue your walk of faith you have a fuller understanding of who Holy Spirit is and how to access His presence in your life. Engaging Holy Spirit's assistance will help you navigate your current season and into your next. Before we get into accessing His assistance, we must know more about who He is.

Understanding Holy Spirit

Remember, I shared with you about the ancient Word of God a few chapters back? In that chapter, I discussed how the Lord sent His Word in advance, and how much of it is still being fulfilled in our lives today. The whole of creation was initiated by the Word of God. John 1:1 says, "In the beginning was the Word, and the Word was with God, and the Word was God."

Holy Spirit was with God in the beginning too. Genesis 2:7 reads, "Then the LORD God formed a man from the dust of the ground and breathed into his nostrils the breath of life, and the man became a living being." *Ruach* is the Hebrew word for the breath placed into man at the start of creation. Ruach is the breath, wind, or essence of God. Ruach is His Spirit and breath that sustain our life. Holy Spirit has been with us since the beginning when God first breathed into man!

We experience the breathing of Holy Spirit again in John 20:21–22, "Again Jesus said, 'Peace be with you! As the Father has sent me, I am sending you.' And with that he breathed on them and said, 'Receive the Holy Spirit.'"

In those two scriptural instances we come to know two characteristics of the Holy Spirit: life and peace. A peaceful life—isn't that what most of us want? That life of peace is entirely within reach once we access and activate Holy Spirit. Activation begins with asking.

Holy Spirit Is Accessible

Asking for help is often considered a sign of weakness and inadequacy. Or we're afraid of asking for help because we believe that something is going to be expected of us in return. However, Holy Spirit was sent specifically to help us. He is accessible, ready to assist us. We'll never live in the jaw-dropping realities of God's goodness without His help!

Because Holy Spirit lives within us, we can look inwardly for His help. Pastor Kenneth Hagin shared it this way: "If you are born again, the Holy Spirit is living and abiding in your spirit."[1] He went on to explain, "The Holy Spirit is abiding in your spirit. It is your spirit that picks up these things from the Holy Spirit and then passes them on to your mind by an inward intuition, or inward witness."

We see this inward dwelling confirmed throughout Scripture:

> The world cannot accept him, because it neither sees him nor knows him. But you know him, for *he lives with you and will be in you.*
>
> John 14:17, emphasis added

> Jesus replied, "Anyone who loves me will obey my teaching. My Father will love them, and we will come to them and *make our home with them.*"
>
> John 14:23, emphasis added

> Don't you know that you yourselves are God's temple and that *God's Spirit dwells in your midst?*
>
> 1 Corinthians 3:16, emphasis added

Because Holy Spirit as an inward witness, we don't need outsiders to access Him. We don't need a priest as a go-between like in the Old Testament and in some other religions. And we also don't need man to serve as our conviction, creating unnecessary anxiety like what I experienced as a new believer. Holy Spirit is accessible; we've got direct access!

With this inward access to Holy Spirit, we can never escape from His presence. Like the psalmist, we may ask, "Where can I go from your Spirit? Where can I flee from your presence?" (Psalm 139:7). But it's a rhetorical question—we can't run or hide!

There used to be times as I walked out my faith when I wanted to just get out of my own skin. I wanted to be anywhere but where and who I was. I wanted to do wrong. I wanted the freedom to choose my own way, but over time I kept getting gut checks. My body would feel thrown off and I would say things like "I need to take a drive to clear my head." I'd say I needed some alone time and exit. But what happens when you're looking to get away, but you can't escape the feeling?

I learned that it was Holy Spirit dwelling in and around me. It wasn't that I could no longer do the things I wanted. It was more about how comfortable the Spirit within me was or wasn't doing those things. We have free will; obeying my flesh was an option. But I got uncomfortable trying to take Holy Spirit to some of my old hangouts. Holy Spirit being accessible to me was deepening our relationship. Things were starting to get personal.

To this day, Holy Spirit continues to convict me. One spring day, I was riding in the car with my sunroof open. It was the perfect day to blast some of that good '90s R&B; you know—the sound of sunshine. And as I got into a groove, the lyrics started to get a bit chaotic. Holy Spirit gave me a nudge with two choices: switch to gospel or ride in silence. I didn't want to close my sunroof, and blasting gospel was not the move in the moment. I opted for riding in silence and ended up reflecting on the goodness of God anyway.

Another time, I was popping out of the car feeling real cute with a little extra skin showing. Holy Spirit politely got me together; I needed to close one more blouse button at the top before I walked into where I was going.

I'm sharing these stories because I want you to see how smooth the encounters of walking with the Lord can be. It's personal conviction based on an internal, intimate relationship. It encompasses honor and access. No one told me to turn the raucous music off. No one condemned me for showing too much skin. I simply wanted to honor the Holy Spirit's presence within me. The second part of Luke 12:48 reminds us, "From everyone who has been given much, much will be demanded; and from the one who has been entrusted with much, much more will be asked." So the more access we have to the Holy Spirit, the more our actions will change in His presence.

Most of us plan our outfits based on where we are going. What we wear to a beach is likely not the same thing we'd wear to visit a palace. Our access changes our appearance, our approach, and our actions. And not because we are being forced to but because we choose to honor the access we have been given.

How to Access the Holy Spirit

When we have keys or a VIP pass to a place, we don't wait in line. We sidestep the line with the authority the keys or pass bestow on us. Similarly, having access to Holy Spirit means we can take a different approach when it comes to our needs. We can make our requests known (Philippians 4:6) with an expectation that He'll answer (Psalm 34:17).

Here's a secret: There's no complicated formula for accessing Holy Spirit. We must meet two requirements; I imagine that you're at least halfway there already!

The first requirement for accessing the Holy Spirit is to ask and accept Jesus as Lord and Savior. Let me slow down for a minute. I want to rush to give you the keys to accessing the Holy Spirit. But I know God has blessed me with a multitude of people who support my ministry and follow me on social media. I love all my peeps, including those who aren't saved. Friend, if that's you, know salvation through Jesus Christ is the best decision you'll ever make—but especially in a season of darkness.

A benefit of salvation is access to His Spirit. In John 16:7, Jesus says, "But very truly I tell you, it is for your good that I am going away. Unless I go away, the Advocate will not come to you; but if I go, I will send him to you." Jesus said that access to the Holy Spirit is for our good. If Jesus thinks so highly of Holy Spirit that He left so that we could experience Him, then that must mean we need to figure out how to access Holy Spirit. Jesus promised that Holy Spirit would come to help teach and remind us of the things that have been said (John 14:26). What a promise!

The second requirement for accessing the Holy Spirit is to ask for help. For some of us, that's easier said than done—especially when we wrestle with what and how to pray. But there's good news: When we don't know what to ask for, we don't have to hide or hesitate. "Do not be like them, for your Father knows what you need before you ask him" (Matthew 6:8), And if that's not enough, "In the same way, the Spirit helps us in our weakness. We do not know what we ought to pray for, but the Spirit himself intercedes for us through wordless groans" (Romans 8:26).

God knows what we need. Holy Spirit knows what to pray. Accessing Holy Spirit by asking can be as simple as "Holy Spirit, help me." We don't have to struggle and keep failing when we have access to a helper. We can literally invite Holy Spirit into our day. We can involve Him in our decision-making.

Accessing Holy Spirit is about trusting that His discernment will lead us into truth. The ancient Word locks it in like this: "But when he, the Spirit of truth, comes, he will guide you into all the truth. He will not speak on his own; he will speak only what he hears, and he will tell you what is yet to come" (John 16:13).

We have a personal relationship granting us access to truth. The Spirit of God is around us, with us, *in us*. He lives in us, not merely to help us speak in tongues. But most people limit Holy Spirit's role to helping us speak in unknown tongues. They stop at that level or give up trying to advance when they can't speak in tongues. Speaking in tongues is a gift that's given freely.

Accessing Holy Spirit is not just speaking in tongues, but rather a way of experiencing full, abundant life. I don't believe we should stop pursuing communion with Holy Spirit after being filled with the gift of speaking in tongues. Tongues is the language; however, we should continue to commune with the very Person of Holy Spirit so we are able to access the full dispensation of Him in our lives.

The Full Dispensation of the Holy Spirit

Two simple actions provide access to the full dispensation of Holy Spirit: salvation and prayer. If you're like I was when first receiving the revelation of Holy Spirit, then you're asking, What is the full dispensation of Holy Spirit if not just speaking in tongues? I'm glad you asked! I found this definition in the ancient word of Isaiah:

> The Spirit of the LORD will rest on him—the Spirit of wisdom and of understanding, the Spirit of counsel and of might, the Spirit of the knowledge and fear of the LORD.
>
> Isaiah 11:2

The full dispensation of Holy Spirit consists of wisdom and understanding. We receive access to the counsel of God through Holy Spirit. Wisdom, along with life and peace, was with God in the beginning. The full dispensation of the Spirit also includes knowledge and fear of the Lord. So much more than just speaking in tongues! Love and self-discipline (2 Timothy 1:7) are added to us by Holy Spirit's presence. We receive power (Acts 1:8) when the Holy Spirit comes on us.

Romans 8:1–17 becomes our portion when we accept the full dispensation of Holy Spirit. I get excited when I realize that the full dispensation of Holy Spirit comes with trustworthy testimony that we are children of God (v. 14) and we are heirs of God and joint-heirs with Jesus (v. 17). It's not all about suffering; we get to share in His glory! We get to live in the jaw-dropping realities of God's goodness.

Holy Spirit Activation

Preparing for the jaw-dropping goodness of God is really about being in position to receive from Him. In a few chapters we'll talk about what it looks like to stand under an open heaven. But for now, it's more important that you position yourself for Holy Spirit to activate in your life.

One of my favorite texts on the unique relationship between man and Holy Spirit is Benny Hinn's *Good Morning, Holy Spirit*. Pastor Hinn shares how activating Holy Spirit doesn't really happen through prayer requests, it occurs through fellowship: "Fellowship is much more personal. 'How are you today? Let's have breakfast together!' That's fellowship. Remember, there are no selfish requests in fellowship—just friendship, love, and communion."[2]

My understanding and activation of Holy Spirit in my life changed when I read this. No begging. No weird questioning. Simple conversation. I can just talk to Him. I can simply invite Him into my day. And so can you.

Again, we have internal access to Holy Spirit. Because we now know that Holy Spirit lives within us, we understand that part of the preparation for experiencing God's goodness is an inside job. Holy Spirit is in us, but our mindset must be in alignment too. The more we are intentional about our awareness of His presence, the more common it will become to walk in the Spirit. It takes a total focus and sensitivity to know that we cohabit with God. Walking in the Spirit will slow you down and make you think before responding, moving swiftly, or being impulsive.

Holy Spirit helps you make right decisions. You will literally weigh every decision and thought on how Holy Spirit feels. The more you do that, the more you will be led by the Spirit of God, which will change everything about your life. This realm is not for those who put on a form of godliness and deny the power (2 Timothy 3:5).

This is the place where the power of God leads and guides you into all truth. Holy Spirit will begin to lead you. I have allowed Holy Spirit to fully lead me, and He has set things in motion in my life. That is how I was able to survive the darkness in my life. I reached for Holy Spirit, accessed His language, and allowed the power of God to fully shift my life. I was able to gain the wisdom I needed to make the right decisions during darkness.

When I had no understanding of my lowest season, the Spirit of God gave me understanding that *it will be God or it will be God*. Holy Spirit released the revelation of a win-win situation over my life. I was able to see the deaths of my grandmother and mother through the lens of the Spirit. I was able to access might, which gave me supernatural strength to continue to live and complete my earthly assignment. The might of God gave me the ability to get up and live when everything in me felt like life was over.

I was able to access the counsel of God and receive supernatural therapy to help me navigate my emotions by separating my humanity from my spirit. Friend, my experience does not mean you shouldn't seek therapy from a licensed mental health practitioner. Doing so may help you while in a dark place. But know this: There is a supernatural dimension of therapy available to believers. Holy Spirit *can* release the right mentality and attitude over your life in your darkest hour. The right mentality is one of believing it's a win-win situation. In the next chapter we'll dig into what it means to adopt a win-win attitude.

PROPHETIC DECREE

I declare the Spirit of God will come upon you now in the name of Jesus. I declare that the Helper will assist you with fulfilling your purpose and destiny. I declare you will cultivate an intimate relationship with the Spirit of God, and the same power that raised Jesus Christ from the dead will arise in you.

I declare Holy Spirit will lead and guide you into all truth. He will partner with you and assist you with troubleshooting through life. Holy Spirit will be the go-to person, be the friend, be the liaison between heaven and earth, be the support system. Be the very One who has the power and authority to ensure that destinies are fulfilled in the earth. Holy Spirit, thank You for being a gentleman. I call on You now.

I declare the Spirit of God will assist, and destiny angels are released to help partner with the fulfillment of your destiny.

I declare the Helper is the facilitator of your destiny in the earth, and your help is on the way. He is your advocate, intercessor, counselor, and much more. He is the one who will give you the might that you need to finish strong. He gives the wisdom, knowledge, understanding, and everything else you need to be productive in the earth.

I declare Holy Spirit will help you be successful.

I declare the same Spirit that raised Jesus from the dead will be in you.

7

ADOPT A WIN-WIN MINDSET

I QUIT MY JOB IN 2016 with no plan B. I was back living with my mom and asking myself daily, "What could go right?" This mindset pushed me to believe in my vision and trust God for the provision. Believing and trusting didn't look like inaction, but quite the opposite, I had work to do. After quitting my job, I took the next action of obedience. Each day I wrote. Those writings became my first book, *From Point Guard to Prophet*, and I used my last check to fund it. God blew on my obedience.

What could go right? was the mindset shift I needed to choose obedience over fear and comfort. I literally wrote my way out of poverty. Today, my previous salary is equal to my annual tithes.

God's goodness continues to amaze me. And it will amaze you too if you're brave enough to obey God. When we are making our way toward God's jaw-dropping goodness, we know that there will be challenges and troubles. However, we are encouraged to be brave and courageous because Jesus has already overcome the world (John 16:33).

Here's the thing, friend: Bravery and courage require a particular mindset to take action. Advancing toward the promise requires a win-win mindset. We cannot approach the grandeur God has for us with timidity. Instead, we are admonished to let this mind be in us that is also in Christ Jesus (Philippians 2:5). That's the revelation! Jesus came to earth with purpose in mind—salvation, healing, deliverance. No matter what He faced, He remained focused on accomplishing that for which He was sent. We must be the same in our pursuit.

In Isaiah 55:11 we are reminded that God's Word will not return empty, but it will accomplish what He desires and achieve the purpose for which it was sent. This Scripture is the revelation for us that the outcome is already set. It's fixed. We were made from the Word, so we can't return empty. We have to accomplish what He desires. We must achieve our purpose. We are in pursuit of the Word that has already been sent ahead of us. That Word can't fail either. It's got to sustain until it's accomplished. We were made from the Word, and we are going after the Word!

This chapter, and the entire book for that matter, is a challenge not to depend on your own understanding. Sometimes it's difficult to understand the sovereignty of God. We have been convinced by the world that we need to process everything. That's not true for believers. Though we are in this world, we don't have to be of it (John 17:14–17). We don't have to process anything. We simply have to trust God.

Proverbs 3:5–6 gives it to us like this: "Trust in the LORD with all your heart and lean not on your own understanding; in all your ways submit to him, and he will make your paths straight." In all ways and all situations, not just for religion and church, we are required to activate our total faith and dependence on God. By walking in the Spirit, not being led by the flesh, we can be confident that we're going to win. Our mindset when rooted in the Spirit is one of victory. It's a win-win mindset.

Win-Win Mindset

I learned the concept of having a win-win mindset in my early basketball days. Every time we stepped on the court, we had to have the mindset of victors in order to play to win.

However, the win-win moved from sports cliché to lifestyle when my mother was dying. The medical team shared there was nothing that could be done for her condition at a certain point. Nonetheless, I tried to figure out a plan B. Where could we go? Who else could we see? What are the second, third, and fourth opinions?

Holy Spirit arrested my heart with a question that would trump all the others: What do you believe? I believed that God was a healer. I believed that only God could do what God could do. God could never fail. His words and promises could not fail. While those who were in authority told us there was no option, a divine option emerged: *It will be God or it will be God.* It would be a win no matter what.

The world is obsessed with winning. And it's often limited to one aspect of life. The world defines winning as a material success. Don't fall for the trap of focusing on materiality alone. The American dream of a house, two kids, and a dog pales in comparison to the goodness that God has in store for you. The material things aren't winning. That's how we can encounter wealthy, successful people who've attained so much but still find themselves unsatisfied. They know they're still missing something.

The Lord's definition of winning leaves nothing to be desired. His winning includes fulfillment, rest, and peace. Winning God's way happens when you settle on the idea that your future is already secure. Winning God's way helps you say, "Regardless of what's playing out, I trust that what God says will be so, even if I can't see it right now," "Even though I'm going through some adversity, He's got plans to give me hope and a future" (see Jeremiah 29:11), and "Though the promise tarries, I will wait because it has to come" (see Habakkuk 2:3).

As long as our trust is in God, we know that He's going to get us through it, even if it looks like a loss on the front side. It's when we start trying to figure things out on our own that things start to get worse.

When you reach a point where you're trying to look for options, it's time to surrender to a win-win mindset. There is peace in having the faith to accept that anything God wants and chooses to do is right. God doesn't make mistakes, and He cannot lie (Hebrews 6:18). But let's be honest, sometimes we allow our anxiety to override our belief and we start to make things happen in our own strength and timing. Ironically, pursuing options outside of God's plan can cause more—not less—anxiety. Peace is often a signal that we have locked into God's choice and a win-win mindset.

Victory Under the Covenant

A win-win mindset is anchored in security, confidence, and hope. On the contrary, when anxiety, fear, and overwhelm enter the chat, we become double-minded, wrestling with our belief in the Lord's plan. We start to edge our way out of the covenant promises with poor decisions.

I love the story of Hagar in Genesis 16. The plan that Sarai put together to get Abram a baby, even if it meant through someone else, came with a full set of emotional trauma. Hagar was sick of Sarai's shenanigans and decided to leave on her own. It seemed like a good idea, but Hagar quickly learned it was not God's will for her life.

She was on the run when an angel of the Lord came with instructions to return. In the middle of trying to escape a poor decision, Hagar met God and received a divine promise. This moment is when we are first introduced to the concept that God truly sees us. Hagar named the Lord according to His characteristic El Roi, "the God who sees me."

Hagar's story offers encouragement for our dark seasons. It reveals that God knows exactly where we are, even when we run away seeking something new or better. It indicates that we can't outrun the promise of God—ever. More so, Hagar's story proves God doesn't shy away from our toughest plights. That's important to know, as people will act like they don't see us when we're down and out.

Rather, even in the midst of our greatest challenges, God sees us. There's victory in knowing that. Even when we are facing uncertainty, God sends His angels to say, "I see you." God still takes the time to prophetically speak into our destiny. You may be like Hagar, trying to get out of something. However, God has sent an ancient word that cannot be reversed. He sees your situation. When you rest on the situation, you're providing an opportunity for Him to show up, reveal Himself, and give you victory through it.

That's what I discovered during the dark last days of my mama's health crisis. I knew that if we were to take my mother off the ventilator, the likelihood of her survival would be low. If she did live, her quality of life would not be the same. I needed to hear from God and asked for revelatory wisdom to do the right thing.

Did you know that all it takes is one revelation to shift the entire trajectory of your life? That's what happened between me and God. He opened my eyes to see that just because the healing wouldn't look like I expected, it didn't mean that she wouldn't be healed. Whatever way He chose to heal her she'd be healed because that's who He is, a healer—Jehovah Rapha.

When we grab onto the knowledge that God can only be who He is, there's a hope and peace that comes. There are situations in which it looks like God has failed or let something happen. I imagine that Hagar felt that way as she fled from Sarai. However, as Hagar discovered, when God reveals Himself and you begin to understand who God is, you can filter any experience through His character. And by His very nature, He cannot miss.

Bible teacher Priscilla Shirer shared an adjusted approach to prayer that really brought this point home for me. She wrote on Facebook, "I enjoy knowing that I can 'make my request known' to God in prayer (Philippians 4:6). But I always end my request with this statement, 'Lord, do it . . . or do something BETTER.'"[1]

Imagine what happens when we shift our mindset to align with the fact that it's going to be a win or a better win. Remember, there is no way to escape victory under the covenant.

The Counterfeit Versus the Covenant

There are times when the Lord gives us a glimpse of a covenant promise that is so glorious that we want it now. We start to believe that He needs our help to get it done, especially when it's so big we know it's impossible. We start bringing people in to help us win the game of tug-of-war. And then we start to experience stress and anxiety. The people we've brought in don't have as strong a grip as we hoped. They're a little weaker in the legs and start slipping at the first sign of struggle. We find ourselves more tired than we were to begin with, trying to pull them along. Sound familiar?

Listen, there have been times when I've tried to make my own counterfeit of God's covenant. I wanted things to be my way, right away. Just like with knock-off handbags and tennis shoes, those things may look great, but they have no value. Or that show where people bring their family heirlooms to be appraised only to find out they're only replicas. No matter how well the item is made, experts will always be able to tell the difference.

The same holds true for our promises from God. Counterfeits will enter the scenario and throw off our focus. In the case of Sarai and Hagar, the counterfeit was beefing with the promise. But the promise still came to pass even through struggle.

When we produce our own counterfeit versions of what should be God's gifts to us, we experience unnecessary struggles. We start to label those struggles as warfare. But I don't want you to think of warfare in the limited sense of the word. I want you to consider that warfare becomes a fare, or price paid, for your choice. When you make a counterfeit decision, you must pay the fare. You'll either pay for the damage or for the replacement. Either way, a fare will be paid.

Another way to look at warfare is through the lens of fairness. Not all warfare is war fare. Some of it is fair war, dealing with the consequence of a choice you made. This is where spiritual accountability comes in. We have to own what we've done and repent. "Father, I rushed ahead of Your promised word. I apologize for not trusting You enough to wait. Forgive me. Teach me how to wait well, not growing weary in the well doing You assign to me."

What Could Go Right?

Even when a counterfeit has been introduced, the covenant will still come to pass. There's an opportunity for things to go right. This is the question that having a win-win mindset prompts us to consider: What could go right?

It's easy for us to see things in the natural and see the worst in them. The seeming impossibility of things pushes against our certainty of God's capability. It's a struggle that we all experience at one point or another. Elijah asked the people of Israel, "How long will you waver between two opinions?" (1 Kings 18:21).

I believe that you are being challenged at this time to answer the same question. How long will you waver between two opinions?

It will be God or it will be God eliminated all other options for me. As a result, I began to filter my thoughts and expectations through God's filter as identified in Philippians 4:8 (ESV):

> Finally, brothers, whatever is true, whatever is honorable, whatever is just, whatever is pure, whatever is lovely, whatever is commendable, if there is any excellence, if there is anything worthy of praise, think about these things.

Here's the mindset checklist I use:

- What is the truth about this situation? What could go right based on this truth?
- What could go right from choosing an honorable response in this experience?
- What could go right if I stripped the moment down to its purest form?
- What are the lovely things happening at this moment?
- Where are the opportunities for commendable and excellent things to come forth?
- What could go right that would be praiseworthy at this time?

I use the Word to filter my thoughts. I recognize that unfiltered and unchecked thoughts will leave room for counterfeit thinking to creep in. My destiny doesn't have time for that! I must have a win-win mindset to progress toward the promise.

Take heart knowing that the counterfeit isn't going to stop your promise either. Adopting a win-win mindset will keep you focused on knowing the outcome is already set on victory. In the next chapter we'll look at moving from having a win-win mindset to positioning yourself under an open heaven to receive God's jaw-dropping goodness. Life hard right now? Know this: It gets better!

PROPHETIC DECREE

I declare a win-win mindset over you. I declare you will step into the mindset that *it will be God or it will be God.*

I declare that you will put your full trust, hope, and confidence in God. He will be your rock and your foundation. He will be the author and finisher of your great faith. I declare that in the middle of a battle, in the middle of a storm, in the middle of the darkest season of your life, you will find peace in knowing that God is in total control.

I declare you will not just read the Word, but you will live and boldly embody the very essence that God cannot lie. I declare you will hold on to God, and even when you can't see your way out of a situation, you will hold true to the Word of God that this battle is not yours but belongs to the Lord.

In life you will deal with issues, you will face challenges, you will be confronted with real life scenarios; however, you will stand on the truth that all things work together for good to those who love God, to those who are called according to His purpose. I declare you will face battles and stand in faith that they will work out for your good.

I declare you will bless the Lord in every season, knowing that God is in control and it will be well with your soul. I say unto you, Let this mind be in you that is also in Christ Jesus. I declare that in seasons when you are required to drink the cup of suffering, you will say, "Let Your will be done."

I release the peace of God over you that surpasses all understanding. I declare whatever you are facing, you will find peace in it being well with your soul because you know God will work it out for the good. Because ultimately *it will be God or it will be God*.

8

GET UNDER AN OPEN HEAVEN

WHILE STILL IN SIN and not yet in my feminine identity, I went to a family friend's house. There were some individuals there I'd never met before, among them a preteen girl who was deaf and mute. Throughout the visit, she would come and stare in my direction. Finally, her mom came to inquire what was going on. With urgency, the girl began to use American Sign Language with her mom. Periodically she'd point at me. Something was up.

Her mother finally said, "You don't know what she's saying. I'm not even sure what she's talking about." Intrigued, I invited the mom to interpret the sign language. She said, "Why are you running from God? He's calling you. God is calling you and wants to change your life."

As her mother interpreted, that little girl went on to share a word of knowledge concerning specific people and circumstances in my life. The mother couldn't have known, which was proof that this message was directly for me. In my unbelief, God brought knowledge. A change was upon me.

When God wants to get His message to you, He'll use anybody and any situation to get it out. My encounter with that young lady was a moment in which I felt like heaven opened up above me. God was pouring out what I needed, and there was no way that unbelief could remain present in the moment. He had my full attention.

Now that you've begun to adopt a win-win mindset, you can be open to believing that as it is in heaven, so shall it be in your life. One of the most important things you can do to activate that principle in your life is to stay in tune with

God's movement. There are times and seasons when heaven is open and your answer, your breakthrough, your launching, your healing or miracle is just one prayer away. Getting under an open heaven happens when you access the ministry of destiny angels and learn what it looks like to align yourself with the timing of heaven. This is when you'll begin to see the reality of "as it is in heaven" bless your life.

What Is an Open Heaven?

There are many messages and methods that teach how to be an excellent entrepreneur. People are teaching courses on how to move in ministry and the marketplace, yet they often fail to include the foundation. The foundation is the Word of God. I used to be confused about my destiny until God shared this with me. The only way you're going to unlock the blueprint of your personal destiny is to come into a relationship with the Word of God.

The Word of God is the secret to discerning times and seasons. The Word of God helps us understand how to partner with heaven and how to hear the voice of the Lord. Being in the Word teaches us how to move in synchronization with the Spirit of God, how to walk with God. Walking under an open heaven is to be in tune with the realm of the Spirit. Under an open heaven we are able to unlock doors that have been shut and shift into new seasons, even when seasons of adversity hit.

My personal and professional successes have little to do with man and everything to do with standing under an open heaven. It's not because of something special about me or some get-rich scheme. Friend, this should make you shout. If I tapped into God's goodness, then so can you! Stop worrying about not being special enough or not having a money-making idea. Trust God's got you. Seek Him and His Word.

140

I don't base my success off what I see naturally; I base my success off the Word of God. I've learned that if I can see it in the Spirit, I will see it in the natural. I do nothing unless the Spirit of God reveals it. And that revelation comes most often through His Word. Heaven opens at His Word.

Psalm 91:1 reads, "Whoever dwells in the shelter of the Most High will rest in the shadow of the Almighty." The King James Version reads, "He that dwelleth in the *secret place* of the most High shall abide under the shadow of the Almighty" (emphasis added). Dwelling reminds us to stay in a place of devotion and alignment with Holy Spirit.

The revelation that I received is that you remain under an open heaven when you are dwelling in the secret place. The secret place is not just going to a closet, locking your-self in a room, or putting on a prayer shawl when finding times for prayer. It's about finding shelter in the shadows, meaning, this is where I reside. So wherever I am, I'm in His presence.

I know that when I'm overwhelmed or I sense my faith getting weak and anxieties rising, I have removed myself from being seated and rested in the presence of God. I'm not covered by His feathers or taking refuge in His wings (Psalm 91:4). I've discovered when that happens, I have to return to the safe place—in His presence—under an open heaven.

The key to unlocking an open heaven is to stay in the presence of God. That's where we'll find rest. The Bible tells us we're seated in heavenly places with Christ Jesus (Ephesians 2:6). Being seated there means we are in a place of rest, dwelling in God with access to the "as it is in heaven so shall it be in earth" mentioned in Matthew 6:10. This happens because the presence of God commands an open heaven.

Getting under an open heaven also delivers additional benefits. In Psalm 91:11, God orders His angels to protect us wherever we go, in all our ways. So wherever we go, we have access to the protection of His angels. Some people have made the concept of angels seem spooky. It's not spooky. It's a place of residence. Because we abide here on earth, we have access to destiny angels to help us.

The Role of Destiny Angels

Destiny angels are used by God to speak or help. They are protectors assigned to be with you, to cover you. We've seen these destiny angels at work in earlier parts of this book. Hagar encountered a destiny angel when she ran away from Sarai. The angel prophesied, saying God heard her but she'd have to go back to Sarai (Genesis 16:7–15). Hagar's destiny angel gave her clear instruction.

Like Hagar, you might be on the run, trying to leave a situation, and you might have every reason to be running. But don't run so fast that you miss destiny's angel giving you instruction. *Destiny angels give us instruction.*

We see another destiny angel in Genesis 18 visiting Abraham and promising a son through Sarah. This time the angel gave clarity on a timeline for prophetic fulfillment. The promise would come to pass "according to the time of life" (KJV) or by "this time next year" (v. 10). Another instance of an angel prophesying with a time stamp is found in Daniel 10:13–14 (ESV). Albeit it's not specific. That angel promised only a vague timeline of "for days yet to come." In both instances, *the angels came to breathe revelation and understanding on what God was saying.*

Another way that we see destiny angels at work is by way of prophetic announcement in the New Testament. God uses angels as assistants to speak and prophesy. This occurs twice in Luke 1 when the angel Gabriel prophesied the births of John and Jesus.

Encountering Destiny Angels

Hebrews 13:2 gives us perspective on encountering angels with the following words: "Do not forget to show hospitality to strangers, for by so doing some people have shown hospitality to angels without knowing it." I am encouraged by this Scripture because it indicates that we don't have to live in isolation, waiting for a big, looming angel to appear and tell us not to be scared. God makes it clear that we can have angelic encounters just by interacting favorably with ordinary people.

God's angels can minister to us in the grocery store, at the airport, or during a walk around the neighborhood. They can be the opposite gender or a different race. They can be wealthy or working to make ends meet. It doesn't matter because God is no respecter of person (Romans 2:11) when it comes to getting His Word to us and accomplishing His will.

What I love about destiny encounters is that God is not locked into one way of making them happen.

Not only can we encounter a heavenly being, but we can encounter angels in the flesh. And now we don't even have to wait on a spiritual being or a big visitation because we have Holy Spirit abiding with us. Holy Spirit, who has both the ancient Word and spiritual information, is with us. And He was there when it all unfolded in the heavens. His job, as mentioned before, is to be a helper. That help today looks like reminding us of the destiny that has already been written and spoken. He was there; He knows it all. Jesus promised, "He will teach you all things and bring to your remembrance all that I have said to you" (John 14:26 ESV).

I get really excited knowing that Holy Spirit has the insight. He shares with us thoughts, dreams, and open visions. When this happens it's a destiny encounter. We're no longer encountering angels; we're standing under an open heaven and experiencing full destiny alignment with God Himself.

Encountering Destiny

As Jesus walked on the earth, everything He did was with the Spirit of God. He always took time to go away, commune, and have private devotion before the Lord. Jesus knew that the presence of God grants destiny access to an open heaven. If even Jesus, the Son of God, needed to take time to access the Lord's presence to fulfill destiny during His time on earth, then how much more do we need to pursue the presence?

Time and again we see Jesus go away and access time with the Father through prayer. But when He continues on the journey, Jesus does not depart from the presence of God. It's the Lord's presence with Him that allows His destiny to be fulfilled and miracles to take place. For example, it's the Lord's presence with Jesus that allowed the woman with the issue of blood to be healed. Jesus' garment was saturated with the presence of God, allowing her to be healed just by touching it (Matthew 9).

Jesus didn't have to say anything. He didn't have to do anything. He didn't have to travel off course to get to her. Jesus was minding His own business, staying on purpose while headed to His next destination. He was literally being and doing what He was called to do. And because of the presence of the Lord, she was healed. He didn't have to detour.

Let's be clear, Jesus didn't have to stop. He chose to stop, but He didn't have to; He still was on assignment. She was going to be healed regardless because of the presence of God with Him. The woman's healing was a byproduct of Jesus having been in the presence of God, under an open heaven. The open heaven that He stood under provided those who passed by Him to have access. And it makes me wonder, If we were to get under the same open heaven, how many people near us would be recipients of the overflow of His glory?

Jesus carried the glory of heaven with Him, and He wasn't hoarding it either. Jesus was walking to His next assignment, another place of purpose, and the woman was healed. The anointing on Him was so heavy it immediately released a healing that had been held up for twelve years. He was *walking* under an open heaven.

Like Jesus, you and I can make a decision to stay on the path of righteousness and walk in the presence of the Lord. We can walk with the confidence of knowing that, even in the valley, He is with us (Psalm 23:4). We can expect to encounter God walking with us in the cool of the day without being afraid of condemnation (Genesis 3:8).

I imagine Jesus' morning prayer was something simple, like "Have Your way as it is in heaven here on earth, Father." And in that having of His way, the heavens were opened, and the woman was blessed. Not just the woman either, but those who witnessed the miracles of that day were blessed and transformed too. The open heaven wasn't just for Him; it was for the multitudes. Anyone could have been healed, but only one reached out for an encounter to change her destiny.

How to Get Under an Open Heaven

As you're reading you may be wondering, how do I step into this realm of an open heaven? Is it just for Jesus and the disciples or something that ministers and pastors do? Nope. This is what salvation gives us all access to. Standing under an open heaven is a benefit of salvation. Our job is to reconcile our hope, confidence, and trust in the heavens here on earth. We left heaven to enter the earth, and while we're still here, it's up to us to seek God's help to maximize heaven on earth.

You and I have full access to the Holy Spirit and the full counsel of God. You can move in the earth just like Jesus did. This faith to believe is available to you. You don't even have to work for it. *Your first qualification for getting under an open heaven happens through relationship with God and acceptance of the authority that relationship extends.* The authority comes with a win-win guarantee. *It will be God or it will be God* in your life. With that in mind, I want to share more about accessing the open heavens with you.

Moses had the cheat code for remaining under an open heaven. He knew that it could not happen apart from the presence of God. "Then Moses said to him, 'If your Presence does not go with us, do not send us up from here'" (Exodus 33:15). Moses wanted no possibility of failure. Inviting God into their deliverance assured it would be God, or it would be God.

The same is key for us in our day-to-day. We cannot accomplish much, if anything, without the presence of God. If we do accomplish something, it's likely to be unsustainable apart from Him. It takes intention to acknowledge God and humility to accept just how incapable we are aside from Him. We literally cannot bear fruit without the presence of God (John 15:4–5). We must be willing to accept the responsibility of carrying His glory, not just sometimes, but continuously. *Thus, the second step in experiencing the fullness of being under an open heaven is abiding in His presence.*

Let's pause for a moment and take in the fullness of what getting under an open heaven means for us as believers. When Jesus left, He declared, "Very truly I tell you, whoever believes in me will do the works I have been doing, and they will do even greater things than these, because I am going to the Father" (John 14:12).

We have access to an open heaven, not just for ourselves but for others too! You are carrying healing and deliverance by carrying the presence of God. When things don't look quite like you expect, you have the authority to command freedom and breakthrough to manifest. A simple prayer can open the heavens above you: "Your kingdom come, your will be done, on earth as it is in heaven" (Matthew 6:10).

Now, can I get real real with you for this final step in getting under an open heaven? Sometimes our beliefs need help. Then there are the moments when accepting God's goodness and authority feels difficult. More than that, there are situations we face when we don't have the grace to pray as eloquently as Jesus. Those are the moments that bring us to *the fourth action for getting under an open heaven, crying out to the Lord.*

> "If you'll hold on to me for dear life," says GOD,
> "I'll get you out of any trouble.
> I'll give you the best of care
> if you'll only get to know and trust me.
> Call me and I'll answer, be at your side in bad times;
> I'll rescue you, then throw you a party.
> I'll give you a long life,
> give you a long drink of salvation!"
>
> Psalm 91:14–16 MSG

Crying out to God under an open heaven is an act of faith. And we can trust that our cries will not be ignored. God hears us and promises to rescue us in times of our distress. Not only does He rescue us, but He'll throw us a party and give us long life. When I read that Scripture, I immediately began to think about what a party thrown by God would look like. It would certainly be lavish with no expense spared. The fact that it's coming on the other side

147

of a distress call makes it even more appealing. It truly does sound amazing!

Friend, there are many people who have that "this sounds amazing" moment after reading a Scripture like Psalm 91:14–16. They then go all over trying to hear a word that's going to start the party and help them to get under an open heaven. They bounce from one popular preacher's event to the next until they receive a "now" word. But when they get home the truth hits; they don't have the capacity to tarry with their prophecy. When the Lord started to talk to me about this, He told me to tell you to ask for the gift of faith. The gift of faith will give you the capacity to hold on to the word.

No matter whether you've been holding on to a word for a day or a decade, it's time to get your faith up. I'm prophesying that there's going to be a season when all at one time the prophecies will come to pass in your life. I believe that you are standing under an open heaven right where you are reading this book. You're not here just to be here, and I'm not saying it to be a cliché. What took some people out couldn't kill you because of the prophecies that are hovering over your head. Heaven is preparing to open above you and dump out the promises. Get your faith up because you're about to bloom!

PROPHETIC DECREE

Get ready to walk under an open heaven. I declare that as it is in heaven so shall it be in your life. I declare Jacob's ladder over you now, and I declare that the angels of the Lord are descending and descending upon you. I declare the stairway of heaven is open unto you now, and I release a God spree over you. A place where heaven is open and God grants you access to as-it-is-in-heaven-so-shall-it-be-in-your-life moments.

Imagine heaven unlocking, and being able to go on a shopping spree where you are allowed to get anything you want regardless of the price. I release those moments over you now. I declare God taking you on a God spree. So I say unto you, get ready for a God spree. Get ready for God to do exceedingly, abundantly, above-all-you-can-ask-or-think-type blessings upon you.

I release an open heaven upon you now and declare that God is granting you everything you need to complete your assignment in the earth. I declare you will have full access to the resources you need to ensure that you're fully able to get your assignment done. An open heaven where you can access the healing that you need, the wealth that you need, the support that you need. An open heaven with unlimited access to grab and go.

The thought is stirring me up: having the ability to reside under an open heaven, where you are able to access everything you need to fulfill your earthly assignment. I declare an open heaven upon you.

9

YOU'RE ABOUT TO BLOOM

DISCOMFORT ROCKED MY WORLD when I moved back home with my mama. I keep coming back to that time because it was a hard season. Prophecies I'd received were not lining up with what I was seeing. I literally had to be uprooted from my comfortable place and go back to a city and home that younger me had left behind. But my return had a different assignment on it. Although I was familiar with my mom's house, I wasn't familiar with where God was taking me when He sent me there.

What I deemed as a setback was really a replanting. God changed my environment to produce a different fruit in my life. And this one wasn't just going to be fruit for consumption either. He was preparing me to add in some radiant, beautiful blooms, all for His glory.

Plow Through Your Criticism

I remember when I first went live on Periscope, I was very insecure. As soon as I made the attempt to show up, the critics arrived. The very first things they talked about were everything that I was insecure about. They came for my gap and some of my teeth that were crooked. And the very first comment was "Get your teeth fixed." It's hard to preach, teach, and prophesy while facing ridicule. But I did.

Then they came for my living space, criticizing the green carpet and peeling wallpaper visible in the live streams. I kept showing up. So did the critics. They kept on highlighting my insecurities. Despite the opposition, I persevered—and

153

bloomed. And one of the things I recognized is if you're going to be successful, you have to know how to plow through criticism.

Perhaps you can relate. You are very gifted, skilled, and talented. You have so much on the inside of you, but you're afraid to show up because you are afraid to deal with it. You're afraid of what people are going to say about you. You're trying your level best to avoid failing in front of your critics and haters.

Dear friend, you can't bloom in that fear. You must be willing to plow through the criticism. You must believe that every promise of God is going to come to pass regardless of what outsiders say. The ancient Word says it like this: "You intended to harm me, but God intended it for good to accomplish what is now being done, the saving of many lives" (Genesis 50:20). This verse is a reminder that in order to bloom, you can repurpose the annoyance of your haters and critics into fertilizer. You are good ground. Your soil is good and worth cultivating. You are capable of being fruitful and multiplying, but you'll need to do the hard work associated with cultivation. It's going to take some plowing. It's going to take showing up.

Showing Up

During my early days on Periscope, I kept believing God. I kept showing up and saying, "Something about my life is going to be different." I didn't know how it was going to happen, but I just had this hope that if I showed up for myself, like I showed up for everybody else and how I showed up on my job, something would change. If I invested that same level of faith, focus, and consistency in my life, something was going to come of it.

Faith, focus, and consistency were seeds that I knew would produce a harvest. I had to keep showing up, even when things didn't seem to be working in my favor. I had to keep showing up on the days when insecurity tried to overtake me. I had to show up after failures, real and imagined. "For though the righteous fall seven times, they rise again, but the wicked stumble when calamity strikes" (Proverbs 24:16).

I can confidently say that I am living in the multiplication of what it looks like when you believe in yourself, show up for yourself, and plow through criticism. When people were laughing at my testimony, I didn't know that God was going to have me use my story to write books and to share it as I traveled the world. Friend, in order to bloom, you've got to show up for yourself, confidently knowing that He who began a good work in you is faithful to bring it to completion (Philippians 1:6).

One of the things I have realized over my years of traveling is that people fall out and shout because they're overly excited by the popularity of a speaker. Then when they get home, they don't have any capacity to tarry with the prophecy. They don't know how to show up and pull the word from the spiritual realm into the natural world and make it bloom. As I mentioned in the previous chapter, the Lord used me to help people faced with that dilemma. He had me tell them to ask God for the gift of faith.

The gift of faith will give you the capacity to hold on to a word. Though it tarry, wait because surely it's coming to pass (Habakkuk 2:3). The old saints knew something about tarrying. They held tarrying services—prayer meetings—where they got together and waited for the Lord to move. They kept showing up, sometimes day after day and night after night. They showed up waiting for signs of a shift.

I'm here to remind you to keep showing up wherever God has planted you until you see signs of the promise breaking forth.

Do you have a prophetic word that's still pending? Wait for it. Are there some words that have been prophesied to you, and are they sort of over your head? Wait. Do you have prophecies that go back more than a decade? Wait. Even if waiting is not your superpower, resist the temptation to move ahead of God's plan. Trust that your blooming season is settled in the heavens and scheduled for a set time on earth.

Psalm 139:16, one of my favorite verses, says that your days have already been recorded in God's book. In other words, there's a prophetic file cabinet in heaven that contains the details of all predestined things. You have to show up and ask God to open up the file cabinet in every word that heaven has declared before time. You have to show up and say, "Let it be so." As you continue to show up, you'll start to see and feel signs of life blooming. You'll begin to feel the shift.

It's Giving Uncomfortable

This season you're in is uncomfortable. Your soul is used to comfort, but the oil of anointing you need for your future requires discomfort in order to come forth. Before you can experience the goodness of God, before you can be trusted with increase and promotion, you must go through a shaking. Growth and expansion sound good, but they are also uncomfortable.

Like a woman preparing for birth, your body will make it known that it's time to shift. "We know that the whole creation has been groaning as in the pains of childbirth right up to the present time" (Romans 8:22). Discomfort comes as an announcement that newness is emerging.

You'll start feeling uncomfortable around people and in places that you've always been comfortable with. All of a sudden, places that used to feel all right will start making you feel closed in. It'll be hard to breathe, and even harder to stretch out. It's like when you just can't find a comfortable position in bed; you can't find comfort in what has always been comfortable. Unlike your bed that's still the perfect size, the place you've been in is no longer a good fit. You've outgrown it. You don't fit there anymore. This discomfort is the evidence of a coming new season! I believe that your discomfort serves a notice that there's time for a bloom, to step out to take a risk.

God is calling you to take a risk and bloom. There are signs of growth even in the weeds of your now season. The bloom effect disturbs and disrupts everything. But don't let the enemy cause you to curse your current place. If you don't have anything nice, lovely, or praiseworthy (Philippians 4:8) to say, then shut up. Friend, is that too harsh? If so, my bad! Instead, simply say, "Though he slay me, yet will I hope in him" (Job 13:15) and leave it at that. Your future is banking on your response to what you are facing right now. You're about to push through the topsoil of your circumstance and bloom.

I believe that discomfort is the announcement that it's time to follow the leading of God. When you begin to have awakenings—seeing sin in yourself, having aha moments— there's something more happening in you and around you. Your thoughts and conversations start to change. Your heart begins crying out, "There's something more to me than just this." Blooming season is near, but it's going to require more plowing, more uprooting, and more discomfort.

Breaking the Cycles of Dysfunction

In order to bloom properly, you have to break the cycles of dysfunction in your life. You must uproot dysfunction and

157

treat the soil of your soul. Otherwise, you'll continue to reproduce what's been planted and taken hold. You have to be healed from the dysfunction that has been present in your bloodline for so long that every time you say you want to get it together, you're reminded about what your mama said about you and what your daddy didn't do.

Have you ever looked in the mirror and gotten mad at yourself because you sound just like her or you're acting just like him? You said you'd never be like them and now you can't figure out what happened. It's a demon called Cycle! It's a generational demon called Dysfunction that has you acting just like them, even though you're going to church. Even though you're shouting and kicking over pews, you've still got some dysfunction that needs to be dealt with. You need to begin to say, "Every curse I've spoken and every behavior I've repeated, I command it to be broken in the name of Jesus."

We continuously talk about the fact that words have power. And we're often encouraging others to speak words of life, but we have to be fully aware of the negative impact of words too. Words create cycles. Words create patterns. Words create habits. Words come back to haunt you. Words come back to torment you. Words create split relationships and create scars. Words create breakdowns in communication—parents can't talk to their children. Spouses can't effectively communicate because of old words spoken in error and ignorance. You've got to break those words off of your life with *the Word*! You've got to affirm the ancient Word over your life and command the cycle to be broken.

In my book *Set Free and Delivered*, I share about breaking generational curses and what it means to be a bloodline breaker. That is where I declared, "The buck stops with me."[1] I included decrees to break the cycle of dysfunction. But I didn't just write those decrees, I declared them. I believe that if there is an ability for generational curses to be passed down, then someone must stand in the gap and release generational blessings.

Cycles of dysfunction occur when we choose to do the same thing over and over and expect different results. If I was going to bloom I had to break the cycle of fear off my life and take the leap of faith, trusting that God would show up in my life. In that book and in this one there are prayers and declarations that can be used to break the cycles of dysfunction. You've got to open up your mouth and speak freedom! Speak deliverance.

No matter how long dysfunction has been planted and reproduced in your bloodline, you have the power and authority to interrupt the pattern. The words in your mouth have the power to resurrect what's been dead for a while. You have the power in your mouth to change what's been dysfunctional in your life. You have the power in your mouth to plant new seeds, "word seeds," as Dr. Anita Phillips calls them in *The Garden Within*.[2] Word seeds like what God used to create the heavens and the earth. You have the power to break the cycles of dysfunction and create a new harvest to bloom with your word seeds. Speak up!

Arise, Shine, and Stage a Comeback

Though it may be dark and uncomfortable for a season, I want you to keep trusting. Know that you're about to burst forth and see the splendor of God. I've been where you are, more than once, so I know that can be easier said than done. That's why I keep a little packet of word seeds at the ready. The seeds are the verses of Isaiah 60 that get me up. I want to share a few with you to help you in your seasons of darkness, buried under the soil and waiting to break forth. They give us instructions about how to arise, shine, and make valiant comebacks!

> Arise, shine, for your light has come,
>   and the glory of the LORD rises upon you.
> See, darkness covers the earth
>   and thick darkness is over the peoples,
> but the LORD rises upon you
>   and his glory appears over you.
> Nations will come to your light,
>   and kings to the brightness of your dawn.
>
> Lift up your eyes and look about you:
>   All assemble and come to you;
> your sons come from afar,
>   and your daughters are carried on the hip.
> Then you will look and be radiant,
>   your heart will throb and swell with joy;
> the wealth on the seas will be brought to you,
>   to you the riches of the nations will come.
>
> Isaiah 60:1–5

The formula in these Scriptures helps us navigate all seasons. It's like the *Farmer's Almanac*, helping us to do what needs to be done to ensure a proper harvest. The Word of God is getting us up so that every time the enemy throws a dart or makes a challenge—stress, overwhelm, anxiety, concern—we know what to do. We've been finding ourselves planted in the Word, knowing about how things are going to work out. We know there's an expected end, and we do our part of planning and preparing.

When I am overstimulated, I have to make the decision to come out of that place by putting the Word over it. I get up and pray. I arise and look toward the light. But when you're lying in the dark and light suddenly comes, you don't always have time to prepare and get it religiously right. We have to force ourselves to adjust to the brightness.

When this happens I can't waste time going through the ropes of religion. I need the relationship conversation, "Lord help me to believe!" I will put the Word on the situation. "Give me the faith to believe" (see Mark 9:24). "Help me to remember that it's going to work out for my good" (see Romans 8:28). While putting the Word on the situation, I'm shining the light of the Word in the dark place. I'm overriding my worry with the Word and giving it to God. I'm positioning myself for a comeback.

But anyone who has played or observed sports knows that making a comeback requires multiple plays. Likewise, we've got to water and shine light on the word seeds multiple times for blooming to take place. Logic isn't spiritual, and my logic will try to get in the way every time, telling me to just stay down when the Word is telling me to arise. I have to continuously cast my cares on the Lord (1 Peter 5:7) and find the strength, God's joy (Nehemiah 8:10), to get up.

The more we practice, the more we experience Him helping us through. Our comebacks become built on the foundation of our history with Him. Our faith and trust are built. That's what helps us to arise and come forth. We can't get to the jaw-dropping goodness of God if we're determined to stay underground with whatever we're going through. We've got to break through the dark soil of adversity and experience the sun shining on what's growing in and through us. We do this by utilizing what we know—Scripture, prayer, and trusting God. We have to accept that He hears us *and* He answers (1 John 5:15). When God's strength comes upon us and He avails Himself to us, we're in position to experience His jaw-dropping glory!

PROPHETIC DECREE

I declare you are about to burst into bloom. You are about to peak, and Isaiah 35:2 is your portion. You are about to burst into bloom and show up on the scene. You are about to burst forth and break out of your hard place. You will be unrecognizable. Get ready to thrive and recover all that you lost.

I declare you are about to excel and blossom. You are coming out of this low place, and God is setting you in a large place. This will not be your own doing, but this will be the Lord's doing, and it shall be marvelous in your eyes.

I declare you are about to step into a time of freshness and a new season is coming upon you now. I release beauty for ashes over you and declare the fragrance of God's goodness upon you.

I declare you will burst forth and show up on the scene. Whatever hard place you've been under, you are about to break out and come forth.

I declare your countenance is shifting, and you are stepping into a time when those who knew you before will say you have really blossomed.

I declare you will walk in blooming health, blooming wealth, and blooming favor.

I declare favor will bloom over you; blessing will bloom over you; doors and opportunities will bloom over you. I say unto you this is your time to bloom again, and the glory of God is revealed upon on your life.

10

JAW-DROPPING GLORY IS HERE

IN 2022 IT FELT LIKE TIME began to speed up. I went from talking on the phone in June to engaged in September and married in January. My life was moving at breakneck speed, and I felt like every time I turned around my mouth was falling open at something new and unexpected. I could barely keep up.

By the spring of 2023, I was sharing lost files of the whirlwind season of matrimony with my husband on social media. All the glory belonged to God as He fulfilled prophecy after prophecy concerning me. To this very day I have to remind myself to close my mouth each time I think about how it looks and feels to walk in His divine glory. You've made it this far in the book, so I expect that the glory of God is chasing you down too.

Following my mother's death, God began a rapid-fire campaign to set my life in order. Her loss had the potential to paralyze me, but God had other plans. I began to experience one thing on the heels of another by way of goodness. I was experiencing a true Amos 9:13–15 (MSG) season:

"Yes indeed, it won't be long now." GOD's Decree.
"Things are going to happen so fast your head will swim, one thing fast on the heels of the other. You won't be able to keep up. Everything will be happening at once—and everywhere you look, blessings! Blessings like wine pouring off the mountains and hills. I'll make everything right again for my people Israel:

"They'll rebuild their ruined cities.
They'll plant vineyards and drink good wine.

They'll work their gardens and eat fresh vegetables.
And I'll plant them, plant them on their own land.
They'll never again be uprooted from the land I've
    given them."

God, your God, says so.

Goodness and mercy were literally chasing me down. First, ministry doors began to burst open. Then, I recorded my first album, *As It Is in Heaven*. Recorded in my living room, the album captured exactly how I prayed and worshiped my way out of my darkest season. I even launched a six-figure digital course!

It was so hard to keep up, but in such a wonderful way. It was as though heaven's and earth's time had aligned on my behalf. And there is no way that I could have ever imagined or thought of the things God did in my life (1 Corinthians 2:9). However, I was grateful that He had provided a few glimpses here and there along the way.

See It Before You See It

There's a popular quote that says "Luck is when preparation meets opportunity." I don't believe in luck; I believe in God. As I continued to build my faith and trust in Him, He began to reveal things to me supernaturally. He also began to put me in situations where I would glimpse in the natural what He'd shown me spiritually. One occurrence stands out vividly in my mind. Shortly after being saved, I attended my first mega women's conference with about sixty thousand women present. I sat in the nosebleed section, unsure of what to expect.

Suddenly, an usher appeared and urged me to follow her as she had another seat for me. She walked me through hallways and tunnels until we reached the front of the stadium. She walked me behind the platform just before the woman of God took the stage and straight to a seat in the front row.

Through my mouth-gaping awe, I was trying to figure out how I got there. How had I been personally escorted from the back, in the booth, in the corner, in the dark to premium seating? Who arranged this? Nobody knew me; there was no reason for this to have happened.

It was God. I heard Him say, *"I just wanted to give you a glimpse of your life coming from the back to the front. This is the evidence, a prophetic glimpse."* That moment would not be the last time that God orchestrated moments for me to peek behind the curtains of His plans for me.

My friend, you may have been catching glimpses of your future all along and shoving the notions away as fantasies not worth indulging. But the truth is, God wants you to see it before you see it. He wants you to see the hope and future that He has laid out for you so that you can be prepared. Where I'm from they say it like this: "Stay ready so you don't have to get ready." As a believer, I think this phrase is an extension of Scripture. James 2:14 reminds us that our faith requires work. We can believe but we also have to *do* something.

The first thing to do is to see it before you see it. Spending time in God's Word and in His presence, you will begin to see not with your physical eyes, but with your spiritual eyes. He will begin to provide you with visions of your future during your time of devotion. He'll show you walking in places and occupying certain spaces, and He'll even allow you to experience what it feels like in those moments.

There's a viral photo of tennis champion Coco Gauff watching Venus Williams play in the first round of the 2012 US Open. At the time Gauff was eight years old. In 2023, Gauff herself would go on to win the very same tournament.

An article on the US Open's website discusses the photo going viral *again*. It includes a comment Gauff made about the photo after winning the US Open. "'I don't even know if that little girl, she had the dream, but I don't know if she fully believed it. As a kid, you have so many dreams. As you get older sometimes it can fiddle away,' Gauff said in her championship press conference."[1]

While watching Venus Williams compete in 2012, eight-year-old Gauff was sitting in her destiny. She glimpsed who she would later become. God will have you, like her, sit in the future for a glimpse at what is to come. However, you must contend for the vision and not let your belief fiddle away. You must see it before you see it, and keep seeing it until you see it. You have to exercise the vision so that when it arrives, you are strong enough to maintain it.

I've told you before, when God shows me a thing, I write it down. Writing down what I'm seeing serves multiple purposes. First, writing the vision is a constant reminder of what is to come. I read the visions regularly. I record myself on voice notes saying what I saw and replay them often.

The second purpose of writing the vision is so that I can do my part to prepare for its arrival. I can outline what I would do and how I would feel in those places He's showing me. Real talk, I might need to consider something as seemingly trivial as what braided hairstyle would help my hair to stay on point in a particular climate. Or maybe I need to go to a place and walk the grounds to get a sense of how God's glory rests on a piece of land.

It's not up to me to make anything happen, but it is up to me to be as prepared as possible for when it happens. That's wisdom from Proverbs 21:31: "The horse is made ready for the day of battle, but victory rests with the Lord."

My third and final purpose for writing the vision is for it to serve as a tracking number of the date to destiny. I want to be aware of when the "order is being prepared for shipping" and delighted once it's "out for delivery." I love to shop. And even though I know what's in the packages being delivered, I am still excited when I get the notification that it's being delivered. I'm the same way with seeing the promises of God before I see the promises.

If God Said It, That Settles It

The ancient word that God spoke over your life must come to pass. No matter what it looks like, if God said it, that settles it. Psalm 119:89 (NKJV) says, "Forever, O LORD, Your word is settled in heaven." That means that as His word has gone forth in the heavens, it is established. He will perfect that which concerns you, and His mercy will continue toward you forever (Psalm 138:8). God is preparing to perfect everything concerning you. The Creator of the entire universe is concerned with completing a good work in *you* (Philippians 1:6).

Until now some prophetic words may have gone over your head while others have certainly been bigger than you. However, in this jaw-dropping glory season, you can rest because it's already done. *It will be God or it will be God.*

There's no more pressure to trust your money to do it. No more sleepless nights trying to figure out how it's going to come to pass. It will be God at lightning speed. Supernatural promotion and acceleration are calling you out of hiding and into the anointing. God's Word says, "And who knows but that you have come to your royal position for such a time as this?" (Esther 4:14). So that settles it—it's your season.

I'm so excited for the jaw-dropping glory to hit your life. You've made it through so much, and you're here to experience His next-level goodness. Here's the thing, God didn't just give ancient words to get us through the hard times. Don't get me wrong, I love a good psalm to accompany me through times of lament. But these Scriptures about His jaw-dropping goodness hit differently. He said that His blessings will make us rich and add no sorrow (Proverbs 10:22).

We don't have to accept a blessing and be constantly looking around for when the other shoe is going to drop. We don't have to hold our breath wondering when the clock is going to strike, ending our Cinderella moment. God said blessing with no sorrows. That settles it, there will be no sorrow with the outpouring of His glory in this season.

This moment is so much bigger than you could have anticipated.

You spent a lot of time in the last season trying to explain things to people who weren't on the same level. Your response in this season is "God said it, that settles it. *It will be God or it will be God.*" We serve a relentless, committed God. His words cannot fail, so He gives assignments to the heavenly beings to bring His creation to pass. Whatever He has shown you—multimillionaire, bloodline breaker, author, business leader, family nurturer—it will be God.

Everything about you and your swag is about to change. Your presence and actions must reflect what has already been settled in the Spirit. It will be done. This is the last season that you'll be insecure because people don't know your name. Let this be the last season you allow yourself to be disrespected because people are familiar with you. Friend, it's about to get ridiculously good, and I want you to be ready.

Permission to Do the Ridiculous

In an earlier chapter we talked about "as it is in heaven," but have you truly stopped to think about what it's like in heaven? The book of Revelation paints a picture for us, but I think those words probably pale in comparison to the actual experience of heaven's splendor. I've had the chance to visit some beautiful places with breathtaking views. And each time I say to myself, "Heaven must be something ridiculous if it outdoes this."

Before we go on, I want to take a brief pause right here. I want you to consider the most opulent gesture or experience you can imagine. Don't limit yourself to just material things either. I want you to really ponder deeply the most extreme experience of peace you can imagine. Now take that same thought and feeling and consider how ridiculously greater it must be coming directly from heaven.

Friend, that's what God's desire is for you—that's the manifestation of exceedingly, abundantly. And that abundance is available to you under an open heaven. By simply believing, you're opening up a supernatural season.

When it's your time, everything you need will find you! Every door you've been waiting for will open. You won't have to look for anything; God will send you everything you need. I can tell you this with confidence because of how I've experienced it. His ridiculous favor over my life reached a height where people would ask, "What are you doing in this season?" My only reply was "I don't know because it will be God." Let me encourage you today that it will be God and it's about to happen all at once!

Record-Breaking Speed and Momentum

Earlier I shared how quickly God blew my mind. But I want to zoom in a little closer on the jaw-dropping season of my life. Even capturing it here made my head spin a little bit.

My dark season ended when the *it will be God or it will be God* revelation hit my life. It was as if a lightbulb came on and He illuminated just how He'd been keeping me. I didn't succumb to depression. Anxiety didn't overtake me. I didn't drown in grief. The magnitude of these realizations ushered in a new wave of glory over my life. God showed me the manifestation of Psalm 18 in my life. With awe and wonder I witnessed Scriptures and prophecies come alive. The Lord Himself stepped into my situation, and things happened suddenly.

I had experienced the Lord through people, prayers, and support. But to experience the Lord directly supporting me was a new level of maturation in my walk. He reminded me that He was with me in the beginning and He'd be with me in this next phase. The ancient Word says, "I will fulfill the number of your days" (Exodus 23:26 ESV).

Then He spoke of my rising new season. I thought that meant broader ministry, new connections, and new favor were coming. In my mind I was really trying to contemplate what else it could be. A deeper relationship with Him? An increase in the prophetic anointing on my life? Many of those things did come, but it was my marriage that truly shattered my expectations. It was as though the tightly twisted rubber band around my love life had been forcefully released due to the momentum.

I'm a very careful woman, even more so because of my past lifestyle. As a single woman in ministry, I didn't have the freedom of mixing and mingling in the way that others might. In January 2022 I dreamed that I met a guy and we became best friends. In the dream we explored new places together and quickly built a connection. In the dream I didn't even recognize the sound of my laughter. It was so light and free.

The man said, "I'm in love with you." Without hesitation I replied, "Well, we might as well go together."

"We might as well get married," he stated. The dream was so realistic that I woke up joyful as if I was already living it. I wrote it down. I also shared it with two people so that when it came to pass, we'd all be reminded that I saw it before I saw it.

The next month during my quarterly meeting with my mentees, three married couples came to me with some version of a marriage message. "Marriage is coming." "This is the last of your single season." Now, I typically rejected those types of prophecies because I felt like people were speaking those words simply because of my singleness. I was self-rejecting the word of the Lord, unsure how it could be for me. However, that day I was reminded of the dream. "I receive that," I said, smiling.

The couples asked to take a picture with me in the middle as a seed that the next time we took the picture, the fruit would be me with my spouse. I obliged, this time with belief, because the dream had been so real. As I drove back home I said a quick prayer of surrender. "If this is Your word, let it be true. Help me because I'm ready to be a wife."

Fast forward to June of the same year and I was introduced to my now husband. We had our first phone call on June 11, becoming instant best friends. I was invited to Houston on June 24 for the WOW Conference, hosted by a friend. After the service, Tommy shared with me he had a date planned for us. I was super excited while I changed clothes after the service and prepared for the date. Since I was traveling the next morning, I wanted to be sure we had a chance to spend time together.

Tommy had made a dinner reservation at a fancy restaurant. He had the menus customized with our initials on them along with the words "first date" and "June 24, 2022." He said he came in advance, got the menus, and took them to Office Depot to get them personalized. He was very intentional and prepared. He then presented me with a gift and a bag full of rose petals. I was completely in awe. He was a perfect gentleman the entire date while we talked and continued to get to know one another. After the date, he dropped me off and gave me a hug and a kiss on the forehead.

Before leaving the region the following day for my next assignment, I sowed a seed—financial blessing—into the pastors and thanked them for inviting me. I also told them I was sowing the seed as a prophetic act because I wanted to experience "wow" in my life.

As I finished preaching at my next assignment in North Carolina, I got a text from Tommy asking if I could talk. He then called me, and that's when my wow happened. "I'm in love with you," he said.

"We might as well go together," I responded. Then it hit me: It was the *exact* scenario from my dream. I knew at that point that he would be my husband. God had said it, I'd seen it, and it was settled. That would have been good enough for me. But wouldn't you know the momentum had mounted so much that God couldn't just stop there.

In September, I hosted the Glory After This Continued conference in Chicago. On the evening of the 29th, I was on stage introducing Apostle John Eckhardt as he came to bring the word. As we hugged, out of the corner of my eye I noticed Tommy holding flowers. His face was serious. The music changed, and I was thrust into the moment of "We might as well get married."

Long story short: I left the conference that night as more than the host. I was a fiancée! We were married on January 7, 2023. Since then, we've been living out the prophecy we received that day to be on a forever honeymoon. At the time of my writing this, we're about to hit the two-year mark. And we've been living in the full reassurance of the love, happiness, and bliss God promised.

I chose this one example because it's the one that surprised me the most. However, I'd be remiss not to mention that there were a number of other blessings that God simultaneously dropped into my life. When I let down my nets of belief, God truly delivered net-breaking abundance. Just like He did in Luke 5: "And when they had done this, they caught a great number of fish, and their net was breaking. So they signaled to their partners in the other boat to come and help them. And they came and filled both the boats, so that they began to sink" (Luke 5:6–7 NKJV).

The key in this Scripture wasn't that the Lord delivered one big fish or miracle. He delivered a volume of fish to turn the fishermen's situation around. It's easy to connect with the monetary and external blessings. But there are so many more that He offers us. I don't want you to miss the momentum and mass that are being built in the seemingly small things (Zechariah 4:10). Those little fish add up to boat-sinking experiences. The jaw-dropping blessings are the daily benefits and rewards that come from God. They are the ones that we sometimes ignore. However, if we started to take a detailed inventory, we'd really see how the small measures build speed and momentum toward the big ones:

- A car almost hit me, but God kept me alive. I'll live to see the victory.
- I was denied access to this place; turns out I was kept from harm's way simply by being absent.
- I didn't go off at the family gathering like I used to, and my nephew asked me about salvation that day.

The seemingly small rewards from God are the ones that bring solutions to challenges and deliverance in difficulty. The seemingly small reward of being able to climb the stairs in your building made way for divine healing to take place in your bloodline, no more heart disease. God is a rewarder of those who diligently seek Him (Hebrews 11:6). God is letting you know that He's handling things His way. Friend, let the momentum build because when that snowball effect hits, it's going to be better, better, new, new all around.

Better, Better, New, New

The ancient Word assures us that a greater glory and future is ahead. "This new house will be more glorious than the former, declares the LORD of Armies. And in this place I will give them peace, declares the LORD of Armies" (Haggai 2:9 GW). Remember when I said jaw-dropping blessings aren't always material? This Scripture confirms peace as a blessing. He reaffirms that peace that surpasses all understanding is our portion in Philippians 4:7. Peace is mentioned more than three hundred times in the Bible and more than four hundred in some translations. I can't help but believe that God's jaw-dropping goodness for us is rooted in peace.

The first wave of His better, better, new, new season is coming to you in a form of peace. If it doesn't bring peace, it's not the thing you're waiting on. As you prepare to receive God's jaw-dropping goodness, put on the shoes of peace (Ephesians 6:15). You must be ready to run the race with endurance (Hebrews 12:1), especially as the blessings start to overtake you (Deuteronomy 28:2).

If you follow me on social media, you know that I'm a sneaker head. I even preach in sneakers. Here's the thing: I've got to be ready to run toward the goodness of God at any moment! Like when the glory hits, I don't want to be slowed down and fumbling with nobody's shoe straps. I just want to take off toward where He's sending me. In the natural sense that looks like a good duffel bag and some dope J's—Air Jordan sneakers. I want to be able to carry some things and run at the same time. Spiritually, I need my feet covered in peace and the Word carried in my belly. That's my look for better, better, new, new.

Preparing for Better and New

When better, better, new, new first dropped in my spirit, I had no idea what it would look and feel like. But I had to take a leap of faith. And the same may be true for you at this moment. Your new season will require you to take a leap! Stop being afraid of discomfort and break out of your comfort zone. You keep trying to settle in spaces you've outgrown. Don't keep making adjustments to be comfortable. Your new season is waiting for you to get tired of the old so you can walk into your new!

For me, the season of better, better, new, new brought a series of transitions both figuratively and literally. I've had to adjust my mindset and relocate my home. And the relocation wasn't just across town. It was across state lines. My mindset shift started with a daily declaration that better was coming. Better, better, new, new became my mantra every time I faced a challenge. If it wasn't going to get better, then whatever it was would have to become new. For me there was no other option besides preparing for better and preparing for new.

To this day I stand on the business of new as referenced in Isaiah 43:18–19—I'm not considering the old, only looking for the new. I plant my feet on the promise in Hebrews 8:13—old situations are becoming obsolete and vanishing. I live by the words in Revelation 21:5—I expect new things and write down what I'm expecting. I remind myself that daily I'm becoming new in His likeness as declared in Ephesians 4:24.

No more poverty mindset; it's an abundance mentality from here on out (Deuteronomy 28:12; Psalm 50:10–11; John 10:10; 2 Corinthians 9:8)! Receiving better and new starts in the mind. But we all know that faith without works is dead (James 2:17). So we've got to put some practical work in that aligns with what we're seeing and declaring.

In the fall of 2023, my husband and I received a prophetic word about relocating. In April 2024, the Lord said, "Sophia, I don't want you and your husband to try to make space in that townhouse any longer. Don't try to find another storage spot or build a new closet to make yourselves comfortable. Y'all have outgrown it." When the Lord said that, it gave us permission to be honest about just how uncomfortable we were. We decided to take God at His word.

Nothing in Chicago said "This is it" during our search. As we packed for a graduation in Houston the next month, I casually said, "It feels like I'm going home." While there, we decided to look around. We found an older home requiring a lot of renovations. I was down for the adventure. He said, "Let's check one more." I didn't object—after all, we were just looking to be looking since we lived in Chicago.

We went to a newly built community and toured a model home. I'd never imagined myself living in a new build, especially not after the poverty and challenges I'd experienced. But the moment we stepped in I was overwhelmed by peace, and my husband's laid-back demeanor shifted toward excitement. This was home. If I'd stayed tied to trying to make it work in Chicago or tried to force the renovation process in the older home, I would have missed the next set of blessings—upgrades throughout the building and customization process.

Don't miss your next. Let go of your idea of what is coming next in this season. I guarantee that what God has in mind for you is better than your greatest expectations. So don't you dare try to prepare for the jaw-dropping glory of God by trying to make yourself comfortable. Especially when you know you've outgrown your old space.

Face it: You've been hiding too long. You've been struggling more than necessary. You've squeezed, rearranged, and shifted things trying to make a too-small life fit for long enough. Stop trying to reorganize. Make a decision to shift and to move into better. Yes, even you are worthy of good things. You are called to better and more. But as long as you continue to make yourself comfortable for temporary seasons, then you're just prolonging the decision required to break out of the box and move. Jaw-dropping glory is here for you. God is giving better, better, new, new!

GOD DID IT

From my initial it-will-be-God spiritual encounter in 2021 to the daily decree of better, better, new, new in my life today, God continues to make my jaw drop at the extravagance of His goodness.

For example, when it was time to move into our new home, God gave us clear instructions: "Take nothing but your clothes." My jaw definitely dropped at those instructions, especially since some of our furniture was already brand-new! But we obeyed God. We gave away everything, forks and all. There's no way I could have written the script for how everything played out. By the time the upgrades and special finishes were added to our new build package, our old things wouldn't have been fitting for our new environment. He had so much better in store for us than what we had in mind.

He took my breath away again on closing day, when we experienced a double closing. We closed the sale of our townhome in Chicago that morning and flew to close on the purchase of our new home in Houston that afternoon. We are following the prophetic blueprint of what heaven has declared, and at every stop all I can say is "God did it." None of what I'm experiencing could have happened absent the hand of God. He continues to show me what "exceedingly, abundantly" looks like.

As I began writing this book, my assignment was clear—encourage believers to believe, not just for others but for themselves. The truth is that God's jaw-dropping goodness is not a myth or a fairytale. It's a reality that He's had in mind for you all along. The reality is that His goodness is not just stuff, but it's also about revelation.

Your job is to believe God, to wait on God, and to trust the process. It's time for you to choose to experience God over your expectations. God is returning you back to the original intent of experiencing peace, abundance, and authority (Genesis 1–2). He's settling you not just into the place of being fruitful, but into the place of multiplying.

Believe God

For a year, I kept hearing *"Multiplication"* in my spirit. And God's multiplication showed up: marriage, relocation, and ministry opportunities. With each new thing I wondered, *Is this it? Is this the multiplication He's been speaking of?* I was preparing my heart and mind in every way I knew how for the next phase and new things. I outlined books. I contemplated ministry areas I hadn't visited before. I thought about what increase and enlargement would look like beyond what I was already experiencing. Yet nothing I did seemed to soothe the sense of urgency around the word *multiplication.*

During the fall of 2024 I planned my quarterly mentoring meeting with enlargement and new things in mind. This time I obeyed God's instruction to open the registration to people beyond my mentees and leave the opportunity open for two weeks. About ten people I didn't know signed up.

Walking into the building, I ran into a lady whom I'd never met before and introduced myself. When I asked her how she heard about the program, her reply blew me away. "I received an email that said, 'Multiplication, increase, and enlargement are coming.' I knew I had to be here." She went on to share, "That's what my name, Andisa, means, 'increase and multiplication.'"

Andisa had traveled twenty-four hours from Johannesburg, South Africa. You know I was floored, right?! The entire time I'd been expecting God to deliver in one way, and He blew my mind completely. He literally sent multiplication from the other side of the world to confirm His word, *"Multiplication is coming."* My name was indeed expanding to continents I have not been to—*yet.*

There will be times when God will speak to you and you won't quite understand what He's doing. It's okay to not know. In fact, the Word says that we'll only know in part, anyway (1 Corinthians 13:9). However, I want to encourage you to take the lid off what you believe to be possible with God. Replace it with knowledge that the moment you call on Jesus, reset occurs, affecting anything or everything in your life.

There is power in the name of Jesus. And the way that God sees to release reset in your life is going to exceed your thoughts every time. His thoughts are not your thoughts, and His ways are not your ways (Isaiah 55:8–9). He can, and will, bring out things that you don't even know that you carry. Your job is to follow up your belief with the patience to wait.

Wait on God

As you prepare to experience God's jaw-dropping goodness, resist the temptation to get frustrated in the wait. Typically,

He will speak a word before you're able to see hope-giving proof. Great opposition arises when we are challenged to believe and wait on God when there is no physical proof of what He said. This is when you have to turn off your natural mind and declare *it will be God or it will be God*.

There may not be a trace of evidence in your life currently, but trust He's going to bring it to pass. Tell every chain on your mind and every shackle on your heart to release you, because no matter what, you're going to wait. And know that the first little glimpse of manifested glory will stir something up within you and give you the next infusion of hope to continue waiting.

Nothing seemed possible when God spoke to me about who I would become, my purpose, and who He called me to be. Some moments I was tempted like Abraham to try to bring those things to pass in my own strength. But I resisted that temptation. You can too. You can break the cycle of trying to help God by *not* intervening and messing something up. The counterfeit will come, the wait may feel arduous, but trust the process. God's goodness will locate you.

Trust the Process

I started my ministry online on October 31, 2013, at the instruction of God. I had no idea that my "little" recordings would expand into the global platform that I steward today. I did not know that He was drastically breaking the cycles of familiarity over my life by requesting a simple act of obedience: *"Go live."*

It's true that going live on Periscope spotlighted my insecurities, making me an easy target for cyberbullies and social media trolls. But it's also true those haters heard the gospel. I was living out Mark 16:15, preaching to folks all over the world. And I was having fun!

Spirit-led obedience defies logic. Many times we try to apply logic and intellect to comprehend what God says before we do it. I'm here to confirm that you don't need to know all of the details. Make a move knowing that He's trying to position you to receive something that's been ordained. The process will require a shift. As I look at the sequence of events from 2011 to 2024 in my life, I can see that every shift, including the one when I felt like I was going backward, was for my good and His glory. God was preparing me for goodness.

God has blown on my ministry and blessed me in outstanding ways. I've had many God-did-it moments. But in every single one, I kept my eyes on Him, the one who did it all. As I keep the main thing the main thing today, He continues to do His thing.

When God instructed us to give away everything before our relocation, I was a little nervous. I struggled with trusting the process. My prayers went something like "God, You don't want us to put them on consignment? We've got some nice stuff that can be sold and help us replace it all when we get to Houston."

Admittedly, I felt a little bit like Abraham. He'd given me this new house, but now I wouldn't have any furniture in it. I'd lived a blow-up-mattress life before. I didn't like it then, and it sure wasn't going to work for me now as a married woman. He quickly reminded me that He is the author and the finisher of my faith (Hebrews 12:2) and He was going to complete the work. My role was to trust the process and be obedient.

In the process of getting to God's goodness, there may be a moment in which it seems like He asks you for the promise back. God is not going to renege on the promise. Your life is not a spades game. God is after your discipline in the process. He's after your character development. He's wanting your

185

prayer and praise to continue to increase, not die down. It takes discipline to steward thanksgiving after the promise or miracle shows up. But that's what He's requiring of you. "Devote yourselves to prayer, being watchful and thankful" (Colossians 4:2).

Give Thanks

Before we go on, I feel a tug to pause. If we were in the same room, I'd tell you to look at me. It's okay for you to accept God's goodness. God is good, and He is gracious, even toward you. Especially toward you. It takes trust to believe that God's goodness will be sustained in our lives. It's easy to let your mind go back to past failures and the bondage of familiarity of who you were. It takes faith to believe that God is bringing you through to the vision at the appointed time.

Today I pray for a fresh wind for you to accept the goodness of God, no matter how not good life has been to you thus far. Today you have the authority to break the cycles that have sabotaged your ability to receive God's goodness in the past. You don't have to be consumed with provision, losing sight of the opportunities for praise, devotion, and time to spend with God. God counts you worthy of every good thing that He's got in store for you.

The enemy is trying to bring fear tactics into the chat. He wants you to believe that when God brings a thing to pass, it's going to fail or fall apart. That is a lie. The devil comes to steal, kill, and destroy (John 10:10). He wants to steal your hope. He's trying to kill your active expectations and destroy the manifestation of your dream before it even arrives. Not so!

Let's cancel that right now in the name of Jesus. Let's cast down every stronghold and imagination that exalts itself against the knowledge of God (2 Corinthians 10:5). Let's ask God to reset your mind to only the things that are true and praiseworthy (Philippians 4:8).

In this next season, all glory belongs to God. Everything He is doing is marvelous in our eyes. We will rejoice and be glad in everything (Psalm 118:23–24). As the peace of God settles on you, I pray that you are wrapped in the warmth of new confidence. Gratitude and thanksgiving hit different when they happen in the presence of peace. They feel good. And I pray that you immediately recognize when God's plan is at work so that you can give the praise and thanksgiving that match the energy of His goodness.

God Did It

You'll know that God did it because the things that He delivers will be things that you can't make happen on your own. They'll be things beyond your understanding. God will offer you help. He'll send ideas. He'll pour out favor upon you. Get ready for favorable outcomes in this next season.

Get ready for God to show up in ways that are beyond your expectation.

At this point you've done all that you can do; you've literally read the book about it. At this point you just need a divine push called favor to get you over to the other side. On the other side of your current moment is favor, and favor comes from the Lord (Psalm 84:11). God is surrounding you with His favor like a shield (Psalm 5:12).

Your story is still unfolding. Keep writing what you see even when—especially when—you don't see it. One day you'll look up and realize that what you wrote in your journal is now your life. Your written words are about to be lived out. What takes years for man can take a mere moment with God. Though this book is ending, God is not finished with you or me. We are one moment away from our lives being drastically different.

The full story of what God is doing is still loading here in the earth realm. Darkness is just one theme in your life's book. Wait on God's light and the God-did-it themes to spring up and guide you to an expected end. Friend, I can confirm that what has manifested and what I have seen in the spirit realm are worth every plot twist, cliffhanger, conflict, and setting change. I pray that my life inspires and stirs faith that with God anything is possible. The beautiful part is, I'm just getting started. And so are you.

Friend, welcome to the jaw-dropping-goodness season of your life. No matter what it looks like in the current moment, know that *it will be God or it will be God*. I hope you walk heavy in it, because God did it.

PROPHETIC DECREE

Get ready for your jaw to drop. For your mouth to be left wide open. A time of shock and surprise. Jaw-dropping excitement. A time of excitement and overwhelming surprises. A time when you will declare, "Wow; I'm shocked."

Your jaw will drop, your hands will be on both cheeks, and your mouth will swing wide open with praise. A time of laughter, joy, and total awe of what God has done for you.

You've waited for days such as these when you could simultaneously laugh and cry. Tears of joy streaming down your face, and awe because God has shocked you with His goodness.

Having your jaw dropped is when God steps in and performs the impossible in your life. That moment when you get the shock of your life. You deserve it, we deserve it. The enemy has shocked you enough. It's time for God to shock you and bring you to a moment of radical change. It's time to be *wowed*!

You deserve days like this. This is your jaw-dropped season. A time when you experience what you never imagined happening for you. These will be moments like those you saw happen for others but never imagined happening for you. You've clapped, cheered, cried, supported, and showed up for others. Now is the time for the tables to turn. You're coming from the back to the front, from behind the scenes to the front line. Your time to host, your time to receive, your time to shine.

It's your turn to experience the joy and wonder of God's favor. It's your turn to experience what it feels like to be blessed, and esteemed by your heavenly Father, and supported by others. These won't be common, everyday blessings. These will be breakthrough blessings. Miracles, signs, and wonders. You'll experience a set time of favor from the Lord, and these miraculous moments will leave you speechless, and jaw-dropped.

Go ahead and shout right now. Step into this prophetic word. Receive it for yourself. Your days of shock are here. Run now and declare, "Wow, God, wow." Practice your praise, because your jaw is scheduled to be dropped. Your surprise is now here.

DECLARATIONS

I believe in praying in ways that activate the presence of God and His divine, angelic assistance in our time of need. When we pray the Word, we are praying it back to God. We're not just praying out of our emotions and what we feel. We are praying the answers that He promised and revealed through His ancient Word.

Ultimately the purpose is to stir our faith and release God's promises. Our faith is activated when we are reminded of the Word. Activation prayers and decrees also help us to feel secure in the Word of God. The repetition and verbal release of declarations builds confidence within us. We become anchored in the Lord, allowing God the full chance to take care of things without leaning on our own understanding.

Here's the thing: The presence of God is based on relationship. He's not an ATM or a genie. He is the living deity who longs to be in connection with us. Whether you're new to your walk with the Lord or have been pursuing a relationship with Him for quite some time, I'd like to share my practice for activating His presence in my daily life.

I start by taking a few deep breaths. This clears the space in my heart and mind for my time with Him. I then take time to read Scripture and pray regarding what I've read. During my prayer time, I invite Him to speak. And because I expect Him to do so, I bring a journal into my devotional time. Then I write down what I hear Him saying. That means that I have to be intentional with my time, leaving enough time to not just talk, but listen to what He's sharing. Sometimes He directs me to go back to the text. When this happens, I go back and document the revelation that He provides.

The Scriptures and His messages to me often become the declarations that I recite throughout the day. I followed this practice as I wrote this book, and He shared declarations with me for you. Use these daily or as needed on your journey to experiencing God's jaw-dropping goodness in your life.

The Ancient Word

In the beginning was the Word, and the Word was with God, and the Word was God.

John 1:1

- God watches over His word concerning my life to perform it.
- I will fulfill every word spoken over my life.
- Before God formed me, He knew me, sanctified me, and set me apart.
- No word concerning my life will return to God void and empty.
- The word of God concerning my life will accomplish what it was sent to accomplish.
- The word concerning my life will become, will come to pass.

- I will not worry, be anxious, or be overwhelmed.
- I will put my trust and confidence in the word of God concerning my life.
- Every word recorded in God's record book concerning my life will be fulfilled.
- All God's promises concerning my life are yes and amen.
- Though He may tarry, I will wait on the Lord.
- As God did for Abraham so shall He do for me.
- The Word is hidden in my heart.

At the Crossroad

Whether you turn to the right or to the left, your ears will hear a voice behind you, saying, "This is the way; walk in it."

Isaiah 30:21

- I will break out, break through, and break past all forms of opposition and resistance.
- I will make the right decision.
- I will acknowledge the Lord, and He will direct my path.
- I will wait on the Lord.
- I will be still and know that He is God.
- I will not be denied.
- No good thing will God withhold from me, because I diligently seek Him.
- The breaker has gone before me.
- The Lord makes crooked places straight for me.
- My steps are ordered by God.
- I have never seen the righteous forsaken or his seed begging for bread.

- Everything in my life will fall into place.
- I will seek the Lord and find Him.
- Holy Spirit will lead and guide me into all truth.
- The Lord opens doors no man can shut in my life.

The Dark Place: Glory After This

Romans 8:18
I consider that what we suffer at this present time cannot be compared at all with the glory that is going to be revealed to us. (GNT)

For I consider [from the standpoint of faith] that the sufferings of the present life are not worthy to be compared with the glory that is about to be revealed to us *and* in us! (AMP)

Yet what we suffer now is nothing compared to the glory he will reveal to us later. (NLT)

- No matter the suffering I am experiencing in my life, it can't be compared to the glory that shall be revealed in and through me after this.
- For with an unveiled face, I shall behold the glory of the Lord after this.
- I shall be transformed into the same image from one degree of glory to another after this.
- I declare I shall see the glory of the Lord in my life after this.
- I declare I will arise and shine for my light has come, and the glory of the Lord has risen upon me after this.
- I declare that because I love God all things will work together for my good after this.

- I declare I will receive supernatural strength to complete my assignment after this.
- I declare I will live and not die after this.
- I declare I will receive a second wind after this.
- I declare every angel assigned to my life will minister and assist me after this.
- I declare Holy Spirit will give me courage and strength to continue after this.
- I declare I will bounce back after this.
- I declare I will continue and stay mentally sane after this.
- I declare I will praise, worship, and be even more committed to my destiny after this.
- I declare I shall prosper and excel after this.
- I declare a new song and a new sound after this.
- I declare fresh oil after this.
- I declare new revelation and insight after this.
- I declare new joy after this.
- I declare financial increase in my life and my bloodline after this.
- I declare new ministries will emerge and come forth after this.
- I declare new doors, opportunities, miracles, signs, and wonders after this.
- I declare favor after this.
- I declare a new mantle after this.
- I declare an outpouring of God's goodness after this.
- I declare everything I need to accomplish my assignment is released to me after this.
- I declare the old has passed and the new has come forth after this.

- I declare new relationships after this.
- I declare greater glory after this.
- I declare no matter what this season has been for me, it's not worthy to be compared to what God has given me after this.
- I declare after this is now!
- For truly there shall be glory after this!
- **After this!**

Win-Win Mindset

But thanks be to God! He gives us the victory through our Lord Jesus Christ.

1 Corinthians 15:57

- There is nothing too hard for God.
- I am the head and not the tail.
- I am the lender and not the borrower.
- I am above and not beneath.
- With God all things are possible.
- My God cannot fail.
- Success is my portion.
- God is too faithful to fail me.
- The Lord knows the plans He has for me.
- I have a hope and a future.
- The Lord maketh me rich and adds no sorrow.
- The Lord is faithful in my life.
- Victory is mine in every aspect of my life.
- It's a win-win situation with God because my God cannot fail.

Open Heavens

The LORD will open the heavens, the storehouse of his bounty, to send rain on your land in season and to bless all the work of your hands. You will lend to many nations but will borrow from none.

Deuteronomy 28:12

- I declare Jacob's ladder to ascend and descend in my life.
- I am seated in heavenly places with Christ Jesus.
- As it is in heaven so shall it be in my life.
- I declare an open heaven over my life.
- I shall see heaven open over my life.
- The Lord will open up heaven and come down.
- I have free access to the presence of God.
- I will experience the bursting of heaven over my life and situation.
- The Lord attends to my prayers.
- The windows of heaven are open over my life.
- I have access to the good treasures of the Lord.

Better, Better, New, New

See, I am doing a new thing! Now it springs up; do you not perceive it? I am making a way in the wilderness and streams in the wasteland.

Isaiah 43:19

- Better, better, new, new is my portion.
- I will walk through better doors.
- I will have better health.

- I will have better relationships.
- I will have better opportunities.
- I will have a better marriage.
- I will have better favor.
- I will have better seasons.
- I will have better memories.
- I will have better revelation.
- I will have better days.
- I will live better.
- I will dream better.
- I will be better.
- I will walk through new doors.
- I will walk in new health.
- I will have new relationships.
- I will have new opportunities.
- I will have new favor.
- I will walk into a new season.
- I will have new memories.
- I will have new revelations.
- I will experience better and new.

Praise and Thanksgiving

Give thanks to the LORD, for he is good. *His love endures forever.*

Psalm 136:1

- I will bless the Lord at all times, and His praises shall continuously be in my mouth.
- I will praise the Lord.
- I will give thanks unto the Lord.

- The Lord is the author and finisher of my faith.
- I love the Lord with all my heart, mind, and soul.
- I will praise the Lord for His mighty acts in my life.
- I will praise the Lord according to His excellent greatness.
- I will praise the Lord from the earth.
- I will sing to the Lord with thanksgiving.
- I will extol the Lord.
- I will bless the name of the Lord forever.

ACKNOWLEDGMENTS

I want to thank my family and friends for being there with me throughout my journey. Your encouragement, prayers, and support made a significant difference in my life.

Thank you to my intercessory team and mentees who held my arms when they got weak.

I'd also like to thank my literary team. Jevon Bolden and Kim Bangs, thank you both for believing in this work. E. Danielle Butler, thank you for getting into the words with me.

To my husband, Tommy Wilson Jr., thank you for being a pleasant surprise. You showed up in the right season, at the right time, and have brought joy and peace to my life. Thank you for your love, support, and covering.

NOTES

Introduction

1. U.S. Fire Administration, "New Guidance on Emergency Medical Services Use of Lights and Siren," January 25, 2024, https://www.usfa.fema.gov/blog/new-guidance-on-emergency-medical-services-use-of-lights-and-siren.

Chapter 4 The Crossroad

1. Travis Greene (@TravisGreeneTV), "You can't just read the Bible, you gotta READ THE BIBLE!," March 1, 2023, Instagram caption and video, https://www.instagram.com/travisgreenetv/reel/CpRAEOKDeeu.

2. John Kilpatrick, "A Prophetic Message for Today," February 9, 2013, 5 min., 41 sec., YouTube, https://youtu.be/B-OebFwelVI?si=YdU8YqExhCG5EAx.

Chapter 5 The Dark Before the Dawn

1. Lisa Loraine Baker, "What Does the Bible Say About Darkness?," Bible Study Tools, May 3, 2023, https://www.biblestudytools.com/bible-study/topical-studies/what-bible-say-about-darkness.html.

2. Addison Rice, "What Are Rubies and Sapphires?," International Gem Society, accessed December 27, 2024, https://www.gemsociety.org/article/how-do-rubies-and-sapphires-form.

3. Seth Stein, "Cooling Rate and Crystal Size," Department of Earth and Planetary Sciences, Northwestern University, accessed December 27, 2024, https://sites.northwestern.edu/sethstein/a-small-is-beautiful-approach-to-upgrading-a-beginning-geophysics-course/cooling-rate-and-crystal-size.

Chapter 6 Access the Helper

1. Kenneth E. Hagin, *How You Can Be Led by the Spirit of God* (Kenneth Hagin Ministries, 1978), 59.
2. Benny Hinn, *Good Morning, Holy Spirit* (Thomas Nelson, 1990), 66–67.

Chapter 7 Adopt a Win-Win Mindset

1. Going Beyond with Priscilla Shirer, "I enjoy knowing that I can 'make my request known' to God in prayer," Facebook, April 20, 2021, https://www.facebook.com/GoingBeyondMinistries/posts/i-enjoy-knowing-that-i-can-make-my-request-known-to-god-in-prayer-phil-46-but-i-/308385297310297.

Chapter 9 You're About to Bloom

1. Sophia Ruffin, *Set Free and Delivered: Strategies and Prayers to Maintain Freedom* (Charisma House, 2018), 127.
2. Anita L. Phillips, *The Garden Within: Where the War With Your Emotions Ends and Your Most Powerful Life Begins* (Thomas Nelson, 2023).

Chapter 10 Jaw-Dropping Glory Is Here

1. Haley Fuller, "A young Coco Gauff at the 2012 US Open goes viral—again," US Open, April 12, 2024, https://www.usopen.org/en_US/news/articles/2024-04-12/a_young_coco_gauff_at_the_2012_us_open_goes_viralagain.html.

SOPHIA RUFFIN-WILSON is an ordained prophet called to impact and advance the kingdom of God. As a renowned prophetic speaker, she ministers throughout the world, bringing a powerful and radical message of deliverance.

Sophia is the founder of multiple programs, including Company of Copacetic Leaders, CBK Squad, Speaker Speak, and Multiply. Sophia's authored works include *Set Free and Delivered*, *From Point Guard to Prophet*, and *Feminine Progression*.

She serves under the leadership of Apostle John Eckhardt, Crusaders' Ministries in Chicago, Illinois.

Sophia is the blissful bride of Tommy Wilson Jr.

Connect with Sophia:

- SophiaRuffin.com
- SophiaRuffinGlobal
- @YaGirl_Soph
- @SophiaRuffin